Rarámuri: Freedom at Twilight

Memories from The Tarahumara

Dr. Carlos Maldonado Ortiz

Library of Congress Control Number: 2020916951

HARDBACK: 978-1-954673-32-8
PAPERBACK: 978-1-954673-31-1
EBOOK: 978-1-954673-33-5

Ordering Information:

For orders and inquiries, please contact:
1-888-404-1388
www.goldtouchpress.com
book.orders@goldtouchpress.com

Printed in the United States of America

TO MY MOTHER:

who carved in her entrails my being.

TO MY FATHER:

*who guided me through the arduous paths
of the language.*

TO BOTH OF THEM:

*for rescuing me from nothingness and launching me
into the uncertain adventure of discovering this
wondrous Universe.*

CONTENTS

ACKNOWLEDGEMENT

I want to deeply acknowledge Mrs. Dora Alcalá, former mayor of Del Rio, Texas, for her invaluable help and patience in revising and correcting my translation to English of this book, which I originally wrote in Spanish. I especially want to recognize her great capability to understand and seize the purpose and meaning of the book, and her sincere commitment to the success of this project. Thank you very much indeed.

Endless, bordering terrifying precipices, winding amidst fragrant forests of pine and oak, the narrow trail ascends by an increasingly steeper slope, as if it were in a hurry to arrive to the sky. The brilliant light of the sun cleaves the crystalline air and bursts into a thousand sparkles on the lustrous tops of the trees, where the birds sing wrapping their metallic twittering with the coolness of the morning. Ahead of me goes Marcos, my little tarahumara guide; he walks fast, playing, jumping from stone to stone, with my backpack ceaselessly rebounding on his back, he has insisted on carrying it. At times we swerve by secret short cuts that climb up grades so sharp that make us shiver with fear, *"to get there sooner."* He has taken very seriously the request of his father: *"Take the doctor to the mesa. Also go to Matias's house, it seems he was sick. Take much care of him!"* Marcos is only ten years old.

Normally it is Cenobio, the child's father, who guides me through the ravines. Since the first time we met, on learning I roamed the sierra looking for sick persons, he offered to take me to the neighboring houses, strewn on the slanting hillside. He abandoned his cultivations for two days in spite of being at the most critical season of sowing. On that occasion, when I arrived at his house exhausted and disoriented, even without knowing me, he received me with great kindness giving me lodging and food, treating me with a simplicity and sincerity that left me puzzled. Then I knew one of the most important traditions of the tarahumara: the Kórima; which is not giving alms, as it is wrongly interpreted in our society, but the solidarity with a fellow man in straits to help him solve any problem.

This time Cenobio could not accompany me; he had had to urgently carry his mother to the nearest village, which was more than four hours of walking distance away, to hospitalize her. Assisted by some neighbors, they transported her on an improvised stretcher of branches and blankets. As soon as I arrived, Cenobio asked me, alarmed, to examine her; *"she's very sick."* I found her laid on the floor of her humble hut, with a runaway heartbeat and the lungs inundated by a grave pneumonia. She had been sick for a week, but she had refused to be attended. Even the previous day she made her accustomed journey of about eight kilometers to a stream, to bring heavy loads of clay to make pots that Cenobio helps her to sell, to support herself. She is more than sixty years old and she doesn't speak Spanish; her son translated her words for me: *"she says she can't grasp her breath, that suffocation does not let her walk."* After I injected her, they put her on the stretcher and went down swiftly, plunging into the thickness of the brushwood.

A jet crosses the blue of the sky leaving a white contrail that gets lost in the distance; on seeing it, Marcos exclaimed pointing to it: *look, a "spout"!* He asks me if I've seen them closely, how are they, what size are they? To my answers he only opens his eyes wide with indifference and continues walking. I can't imagine the idea I've left in his mind; an airplane is something of no practical value in his world. Then he asks if I like honey, and moved with emotion he tells me when, together with some friends, they knocked down with blows from stones a *"giant"* honeycomb that hung under a crag at the edge of an abyss; pursued by the swarm, they had to run to submerge in a nearby stream, where they stayed for a long time because the bees *"didn't want to leave."* He says some of them remained all swollen for several days; that the honey was very good.

The mesa is a wondrous place. Situated on the upper part of an imposing canyon, it is incrusted like a huge step in an enormous granite wall that surrounds a high plateau; its other end faces the void. From the border of the precipice one can see, in the depth, the winding course of a river that, on its arduous way toward the sea, flows furtively amongst rocks and ravines, resembling a fine silver thread hidden behind the tenuous fog that ascends from the bottom, turning blue, to the distance, the intense greenness of the vegetation. There are few houses on the mesa. The farthest one is Matias', built at the foot of the rock face, beside a rugged trail that goes up to the plateau by the only practicable pass. He has rejoiced at our arrival; he suffers from a serious bronchitis that impedes him to work. He has not descended to the village to be treated because he's afraid of not been able to come up again *"due to the lack of air,"* and he has no one to stay with down there. In another house a young woman had just given birth the night before; to facilitate the delivery she squatted to have her parturition, leaning the abdomen on a shawl hung from the beams of the ceiling. She and the baby were in excellent condition; at the request of the husband I left her some vitamins *"so she gains strength."* On asking her why she had not gone to be attended at the clinic, I was surprised at the logic of the indigenous thought and their peculiar common sense: *"there they lay you down and then you have to push upwards, like that it's harder for the kids to come out."*

Months later, mounted on a grayish green rock for so much lichen, I contemplated, still incredulous, the intricate labyrinth of colossal canyons that spread over the horizon. The wind and the water, encased in this abysmal world, formed parallel torrents that flowed irrepressibly crumbling the earth and reinventing the space; creating a fabulous landscape of long plateaus bordered with monumental rocky crests, separated by unfathomable precipices that came to sink almost two thousand meters into the wrinkled face of the planet, resembling monstrous throats that threatened to devour the whole vegetable kingdom that, tenaciously clung to the inclined slopes, displayed an amazing diversity, changing drastically as it descended into the profundities: lush forests inhabited by little rodents, heaths in which dwell an infinity of birds, and deer find a refuge, willowy cactuses where vultures rest like funereal watches. As in a titanic open book, a part of the terrestrial life was condensed in the immensity of the gorges.

In the middle of the canyons, isolated portions of land had resisted the attack of erosion, and they rose from the bottom resembling grandiose sculptures carved by the natural elements: a Gothic cathedral, a belfry, a giant's finger, a portentous pillar that seemed to support the sky. Cenobio had told me that some people sow on the tops of these places, mounting to them by rudimentary ladders made of simple trunks with narrow steps carved on their surface. Looking at the dreadful verticality of the rocky walls that circled them, it was inconceivable to me that someone had the audacity to climb them using only the hands and feet, without any protection. For the native this was simply one more episode of his endless quest for new areas of cultivation, which began with the arrival of the Spaniards; suffering since then the constant spoliation of his best lands, what has compelled him to occupy the wildest zones of the canyons. Even at present, the mestizos dispute over the few level pieces of land they own, leaning on certain authorities whose racist mentality is sometimes subtle, but always present and implacable.

The tarahumaras do not live in large communities. The families inhabit settlements dispersed on the declivities of the canyons and on the plateaus, each a considerable distance from one another; laced by innumerable trails that cross defiles and spots of extraordinary beauty, which have been carved through the centuries by countless generations of indefatigable walkers. *"So you let the wind run free and your animals do not disturb anybody"*; it was the simple explanation of Cenobio when I inquired about the reason of such an intricate structure, that has allowed the tarahumara society to develop a singular way of living where, at the same time, the individual independence is preserved and the needs of social communication are satisfied. The families lead a solitary existence, relatively distant from other members of the community, concentrated in their domestic and field activities. Though they frequently interchange personal visits or perform collective agricultural labors in which several neighbors participate, concluding with tesgüinadas of gratitude; only on special occasions, like festivities of a religious kind, they break their isolation gathering in numerous groups to carry out their celebrations in sites considered as sacred.

The abrupt geographic unevenness originates very contrasting climatic conditions; in winter, for instance, the high plateaus and the mountains are covered with snow, while in the bottom of the canyons an agreeable temperate climate prevails. These climatic variations have determined the seminomadic life of the tarahumara. Normally each family owns two houses: one inside the canyons and the other on the plateaus. They reside in the first one in winter, seeking to protect themselves from the intense cold of the high places; during the summer they move to the plateaus to escape from the heat of the canyons and cultivate the flat terrains, profiting from the rains. Nowadays, the growth of the mestizo villages has encompassed lands that belonged to the natives, constraining many families to live all year round in the same place. Few of them still dwell in caves, and it's no longer possible to find the giant caverns described by the first missionaries, which sheltered in the interior rooms separated by walls made of stones and clay, where several families lived together and as they said, *"they seemed more like sepulchers than houses."*

As the majority of the rarámuri families, Pedro's family only use their house to keep their clothes, bedclothes, petates and other belongings; or to sleep if the weather is unfavorable. All their activities are performed in the exterior. Their scarce furniture: a shaky table, four chairs and a double oven made of clay, to cook, are outside the rooms, under a front shed of wooden tiles. They usually build two small rooms of adobe or stone, though in the wooded zones they prefer wooden trunks. There is not a uniform style and everyone constructs them according to their liking and possibilities. In the areas near to the mestizo villages, modern materials and furniture are frequently used.

A serene afternoon I conversed with Pedro and his family in the shade of a fragrant orange tree, in the yard of his house, delighting in a succulent papaya he had cut in his orchard. We talked about trivial and simple things, and, nevertheless, it was such a charming and pleasant moment that I could not conceive a better way to enjoy it. Timetables had evanesced; we ate when hunger *"pierced"* us, and if the heat made us fall into lethargy we slept free of worries. Here reigned the sun, the rain, the drought, the winter. And nobody cared about knowing his age or celebrating birthdays. The familial harmony seemed almost perfect. It was well known that tarahumaras are not in the habit of hitting nor rebuking their children in order to educate them, and I've never seen a youngster grumble to his parents. Briefly I entered the most intimate details of their daily life; thus I knew about the raven that stole Pedro's hat, and how he finally found it after a long time, in the hole of a trunk; or the time when some of his goats flung down a precipice, startled because he stumbled and fell on them when his huarache *"burst."*

On the way to his house I had found a picturesque chalet on a hill by the edge of a ravine; all made of wood, it had a balustered porch, a pitched roof and even a balcony on the second floor to contemplate the spectacular panorama. In it lived a middle aged man and his mother. On making him notice the unusualness of the construction, Pedro smiled and roguishly told me in a precautionary tone: *"that one likes men."* He made me remember the ancient chronicles of the first missionaries of the tarahumara, who mention the existence of homosexuality in the indigenous communities. Then like today, in a reaction that has all the appearance of being completely natural, and that is equal to the one of ten other indigenous groups that I know in México, although there is not a violent rejection toward that conduct, it is very evident that there is a veiled disdain against it and a certain social isolation, in part voluntary, of those persons.

The nightfall came imperceptibly. Before darkness blinded them, the women hastened to unfold two petates on one side of the shed; they arranged the children in the center and they huddled up to their sides, wrapping themselves in several blankets; it was funny to see that tight heap of small and large bulks. Pedro lay down by the oven, after chasing a dog that had stolen that place from him. A little while later they dreamed under the starry sky, lulled by the monotonous singing of crickets and frogs. From time to time was heard, lost in the undergrowth, the barking of the dogs, fighting against the coyotes.

It's been pouring down rain for a week. Large black threatening clouds seem to break apart when striking the hills, gushing tons of water in torrential downpours that last the entire day. Thick trickles fall from the sloped tile roofs creating real water curtains in front of the houses. Few people venture into the streets of the village, filled with extended quagmires, crossing them by hops to avoid the puddles. The terrifying clamor of thundering resounds on the walls of the ravines, and creates a fear that the sky will tumble at any moment. The volume of rivers and streams has increased, copiously, transforming them into monstrous liquid snakes that raze everything in their path. Enormous trunks pass wallowing violently, dragged by the impetuous current, occasionally taking out their branches over the frothy vortices, simulating a last farewell gesture; entering the margins of the torrent, the bold inhabitants of the river banks are in the habit of lassoing them like cattle, to dry them and use them as firewood, sparing the effort of bringing them from the woodland. In this season it's painful to travel the muddy and slippery trails, and it's impossible to cross the fords. Many villages are left isolated and it is necessary to shun the turbulent waters balancing on rudimentary telphers. In some places they have built spectacular suspension bridges whose undulating sway reels the droves of mules that, loaded with groceries and provisions, cross them timorously, hastened by blows of the stick from the muleteers.

With the arrival of the rains the vegetation comes back to life in an explosive way, and the landscape acquires the aspect of a jungle, with a hallucinating greenness. Heat and humidity awaken the papaya, banana and mango trees, which abound in the bottom of the canyons, and whose fruit feeds the chattering flocks of parrots that, like a palpitating green stain, fly swiftly across the cloudy sky. The insects also proliferate everywhere, pullulating gigantic grasshoppers in brilliant colors and exotic arachnids of red and velvety skin. By night the mosquitoes besiege the sleep with their stubborn buzz, and by day the gnats annoy the inhabitants biting their elbows and hands, leaving tiny bloody ulcers that, in comparison to the size of the insect, can only be explained by imagining it as a huge flying mouth. The pernicious presence of poisonous scorpions, whose virulent stings sometimes kill little children, and venomous serpents, like the coral and rattlesnakes, turn the place into a wild and aggressive world.

A tragic event has touched the region: due to the softening of the earth on account of the excessive humidity, the steep slope of a hill has crumbled, creating a terrible avalanche of mud, trees and stones, burying the houses on the banks of a river and obstructing its course, shaping an

unexpected dam that has caused serious floods upriver. Nobody knows how many dead persons there were; a complete family has disappeared, their bodies interred under a mountain of mire and irretrievable.

"People only live where there is water," Valente replied when I asked why nobody lived on the opposite hillside, no water springs existed there. It was like an awakening, never before had this fundamental reality been so evident to me. I remembered it now while, lying on the ground, I drank by submerging my lips and sipping in a crystalline puddle, at the edge of a shady path; its incredible transparency allowed me to see the smallest details of the bottom, on which reverberated fugitive solar sparkles. The water flowed forth softly under an enormous rock covered with moss; it was extremely cold and, on touching it, my fingers got livid, twitching in pain. It is in these springs where the rarámuris pause to rest on their long walks, preparing, to recuperate energies, a refreshing beverage with pinole, mixed at times with sugar. This is one of the great pleasures of the sierra, to satiate thirst with the pristine liquid emanated from the earth, after having mounted the exhausting flanks of the canyons. Absorbed in thought, looking at the water folding while gliding toward a weir, I hadn't noticed a native waiting for his turn behind me; I hastened to finish, assuring him that the water was very good; on listening to my twisted tarahumara he laughed, amused, and rolling carefully a wide oak leaf, he sank it in the puddle using it as a container, then he sat to drink quietly on a stone. Ashamed, I told him jokingly that he should have lent me his *"glass"* so I wouldn't get soiled; he answered, abashed, he didn't want to disturb me *"as perhaps thus you liked to drink."* He said that sincerely, without scoff or malice. I was left impressed from his adaptation to the environment and his conception of the respect to others; they were the basis of the notable harmony of his society.

The existence of water springs is common in the low and middle parts of the canyons, but they are scarce in the upper strip and on the plateaus. During the summer drought most of them dry up, and getting water becomes a serious problem. On the plateaus the people have to share with domestic and wild animals the meager sources, transformed into real quagmires, needing to filter the liquid in pots of porous clay to be able to drink it. I had been walking for ten days by the sierra, visiting tarahumara settlements, and I still hadn't had the chance to take a bath. It was ridiculous to intend to give them sanitary advice with my clothes as dirty as theirs; with the body, like them, stinking of that characteristic smell mixture of stale sweat, impregnate smoke and aged dirt; and with the head, like them, full of lice, whom I discovered an afternoon while feeling their footsteps as they say *"drumming me the roof."* Nevertheless, my worry was in vain, the tarahumaras don't pay attention to those superfluities. In these places, having a bath entails a laborious routine; together with the terrible lack of water, which must be brought from distant places, and chop logs to make a fire and heat it in pails, if one has them. Although some natives have been able to acquire hoses to carry the vital liquid to their houses, the consumption of time, energy and resources makes an extreme wearing down which is hardly permitted by the critical conditions of life of the rarámuri. With the arrival of snowfalls and the atrocious cold of winter, taking a bath becomes a brutal martyrdom.

But this situation is not exclusive of the native; the mestizos of the sierra villages, lacking many services, also last days without having a bath and suffer the same plagues. Only those who live in the vicinity of the rivers, where climate is more benign, have the advantage of being able to take a plunge more often. For someone from the city, who just by turning on a faucet have the luxury of wasting water, the difficulties in the sierra are inconceivable, and it is very easy for them to criticize and despise the Indian. In fact, many citizens also have negative attitudes against the mestizos of the sierra, considering them ignorant, rough and dirty people.

The world seemed to turn vertiginously, as trapped in an invisible vortex that converged over their heads. The woods, the people, the sierras, the sky… The images passed fugaciously, reflecting on the exotic cubic panaches of mirrors that crowned their headdresses of cloths in vivid colors, resembling magic crystal boxes that, on the iridescent revolving of the dancers, allowed sporadic glimpses toward a concealed interior universe. From their vertex came forth a showy ornament of slender multicolored ribbons, descending to the waist, and flapping in the wind. They turned frequently uttering in unison an acute shouting, furiously undulating their long black cloaks, while they tapped on the ground to the timing of a violin, stirring the earth with their boots. They had been dancing the dance of the Matachines all day and night in the center of a large open space, on one side of the church, resting only brief minutes between each piece of music to adjust their garments and wipe off sweat, or to go dance inside the church. The exhausting ceremony was part of a *"tónari,"* one of the most important tarahumara celebrations, dedicated to invoke the celestial help, to implore the rains to appease a prolonged drought that affected the region, damaging the crops.

The ritual had begun the preceding afternoon. With contributions from the members of the community, they had managed to gather a numerous flock of goats, twenty six in all, which would be used as an offering. Throwing sounding spits, bleating uneasy, the animals waited *"huddled"* near a simple squared altar of cement, next to which three wooden crosses were thrust into the ground. Directed by an order from the governor, pulling them with a rope tied to the neck, the goats were led one by one before the altar to be immolated. On having the presentiment of the proximity of death the animals became insane, resisting with all their strength to be dragged to the slaughter place, giving out prolonged nooos that made me shiver, they sounded almost human. But their struggle was useless; two robust young men tied their hoofs with a rope, tumbling them sideways and clenching their noses firmly with the hands to immobilize their head. Then, one of the leaders of the ceremony with a skillful blow cut their throats, collecting in a gourd the blood that escaped from their throats in gushes. Impotent, the animals shook desperately, in a final attempt to liberate themselves from their fastenings, opening their eyes wide and giving out heavy snorts; gradually they got quiet, inert, and the spark of life became extinguished from their slant pupils. Already dead, they piled them up *"topsy-turvy"* on one end of the open space, where several men flayed them carefully, taking care of not damaging the skin so they would be able to use it to make hides for drums, receptacles or huarache straps. Forthwith they cut them up, putting the pieces of meat in sacks and arranging them minutely on the altar.

The weather had been somewhat cloudy the two previous days, but the last afternoon of the ceremony it got worse in an exaggerated way; when the attendees congregated around the altar to carry out the dedication of the offerings, dense threatening clouds suffocated the sky, darkening the day prematurely. The arrival of the rain seemed imminent. Accompanied by the governor, an old man stood in front of the multitude beginning with a very loud and eloquent discourse addressed to the sky; he repeated frequently the name of their supreme god, *"Onorúame,"* pointing to the offerings and raising both hands, supplicant. Unexpectedly the atmosphere got disturbed in a strange manner; sudden gusts of wind arrived raising enormous clouds of dust, forming violent whirlwinds that pushed the multitude, blinding them and forcing them to cover their faces to protect themselves from the fierce dust-laden wind. It was an imposing and unwonted scene. In spite of the chaos, the old man continued talking imperturbable, brandishing his cane energetically, making expressive gestures of complaint to the firmament. A thick cloud of dust squeezed him making him disappear for an instant, disarranging his hair, pulling his clothes and whipping his face. It was as if the wind was enraged and tried to shut him up with slaps. Little after the old priest finished his audacious demand, the wind ceased all at once. It was, perhaps, only an extraordinary coincidence, but those in the audience looked at one another disconcerted, making a vague expression of fear. Once the calm returned, the governor pronounced some brief words in a muted voice, and the crowd dispersed to go eat a part of the offering, that a group of cooks had boiled in two large aluminum pots, without salt or condiments.

At nightfall, several families set off on their homeward journey carrying little bundles of meat from the offering, which were apportioned to all the participants. Nevertheless, the majority congregated on a hill, above the school, kindling a couple of bonfires; to conclude the celebration, they had programmed a nocturnal *"ball race."* Near one of the fires they began to accumulate blankets, bedclothes, garments, radios, a spotted goat that had escaped the slaughter, and even portions of the offering; it was the prize that the victors would win. In the midst of the uproar the two teams of competitors were organized, determining the path of the race: they would make six turns to a circuit of about fifteen kilometers, starting through the bottom of an abrupt ravine, mounting afterward to an oblong plateau, to return again to the settlement descending by the opposite slope. The rules of the game were also set, exhorting them not to resort to sorcerers in order to harm their adversaries. One of them, taking precautions, wore as amulet a deer hoof tied to his belt, on the belief that it would concede him greater speed. The contenders began their warming exercises making humorous commentaries and uttering mutual menaces in jest. A dozen kids watched them moved with emotion, playing, emulating the most competent runners, for whom they manifested great admiration.

The objective of the competition was to conduct a small ball, carved in oak wood, to the finish line, throwing it with the instep the farthest possible. The delicate mission behooved the best endowed member of the team, while his companions watched and indicated to him where the ball fell, so he could throw it again without losing time. The first in completing the distance stipulated would be the winner. According to some colonial chronicles, it is probable that in ancient times this event had had a certain religious character, but, nowadays, it tends to be merely a sports competition. The start of the race aroused a tremendous uproar; the multitude yelled fiery encouraging the teams that, to locate the ball in the darkness, lit themselves with okote torches. The flickering light of the firebrands gave a theatrical resemblance, oneiric, to the unusual spectacle; deforming the athletic figures of the competitors, who left howling as possessed by the devil, entering tumultuously the forest seeking the decisive inaugural shot, which went to hide under a dense tangle of thorny weeds. A while later only dispersed blazes could be seen romping in the blackness, like extravagant igneous beings that, in a surreptitious flight, advanced hiding behind the somber trunks of the trees. The shouting hushed when they went around a monumental rock, whose sharp profile evoked a drowsy giant.

The rest of the night they were passing every two hours without stopping; the public waited for them somnolent, greeting their momentary arrival with ovations of decreasing effusion; tiredness began to affect them. Notwithstanding, the teams continued running at a surprising rapidity; their resistance was impressive after so many hours of effort, since many of their integrants had participated in the dances of Matachines.

In a cruel irony, the following day it dawned totally clear; not even a cloud could be seen on the horizon. The rain never fell, causing the sarcasm of the few mestizos residing in the place; who diverted themselves calculating how many kilos of meat each participant had gotten, considering ridiculous their small number in comparison to the size of the offering. That afternoon, walking by the bank of the tortuous meanders of the river, I found an old man that toiled in building a weir of stones where he could raise the languid little fish that, with difficulty, swam by creeping in the shallow waters. On seeing me he sat to rest, taking off his hat to look, winking, at the burning solar disk. The day calcined. I approached him commenting on the problem of the lack of rain, and lamenting that the sacrifice of goats had not worked. *"No, well,"* he answered discouraged, *"the good God has already forgotten about us."*

Towards the end of the XVI century, motivated by the ambition of finding gold and silver, the first Spanish explorers entered lands of the present state of Chihuahua which was then part of the extensive province of Nueva Viscaya. Though they discovered silver-bearing veins in Santa Bárbara, to the southeast of the sierra tarahumara, and in Chínipas, to the west of the same, assailed by hostile Indians they had to abandon the enterprise, temporarily. Shortly after the beginning of the XVII century, the first catholic missionaries of the order of the Society of Jesus penetrated into tarahumaran territory to begin their evangelizing task, opening the breach that permitted the colonization by the white man, causing a drastic transformation of the region. There were two routes of penetration: one departing from Culiacán, in the present state of Sinaloa, towards the northeast as far as Chínipas; the other, more direct and in the long run more important, set off from Guadiana, the current city of Durango, toward the northwest. At that time the tarahumaras inhabited the large central plains of Chihuahua, settled on the borders of the conchos river from the limits of the Sierra Madre Occidental. Dispersed in hamlets, they lived from subsistence agriculture, cultivating corn, beans and squash, complemented with hunting, fishing and gathering of wild fruit.

In an effort to facilitate evangelization and have greater administrative control on the autochthonous communities, the *"reduction"* system was established in all the Nueva España, which pretended to congregate the aborigines in towns founded around a small church and a large square, which acted as missionary centers. The ecclesiastical authorities considered the living in caves, scattered throughout the sierras, only admissible for the animals, for it propitiated the *"depraved customs"* of the Indians and an existence without law or god that degenerated in demoniac idolatries. Despising their culture and their traditions, they were forced to move to the missions. When they resisted leaving their homes, the church solicited the support of the army, which punished the rebels by lashing, burning their houses and destroying their crops; eliminating systematically their idols to eradicate their beliefs. At times they took the children and women as prisoners to subdue the warriors. Some colonial accounts are terrifying; for refusing to accept the new religion, the Indians were accused of heresy or of being sorcerers sent by the devil, condemning them to the gallows. Many aborigines preferred to flee to the mountains before renouncing ancestral customs such as polygamy, the tesgüinadas, idolatry and living in the country.

The faith and conviction of most missionaries are unquestionable, though sometimes they fell into fanaticism. In the beginning they all came from distant Europe, and many of them were great scholars, graduates from the best universities of the old continent, with a very refined culture and even a heritage of noble ancestry. An enormous and sincere vocation was required to decide to abandon the comfort and shelter of home, knowing they would go to face an unknown world full of dangers, leaving their families behind with the certainty of never seeing them again. At the time, the trip from México City to the Tarahumara lasted more than two months. The muleteers, with their droves of beasts burdened with merchandise, were the few people who ventured to travel the arduous and insecure roads of the Colony, conveying to its most remote corners from the most indispensable articles and utensils to the most superfluous adornments; risking their lives to defend their precious cargoes from the gangs of robbers or of revolted Indians that constantly harassed them. It is hard to imagine nowadays the penuries the missionaries had to bear, living in extreme poverty, often alone, in places very far away from civilization; suffering from hunger and fatigue on traveling the inhospitable sierras. In their struggle to propagate Christianity, many religious fell, shot by envenomed arrows or with the skull shattered by cudgeling.

Unfortunately, trapped in the ideology of their epoch, the missionaries had a narrow and dogmatic mentality, replete of prejudices. For them the sole correct way of living life and religion was in conformance with the European model; they never conceived that Christianity, even without deviating from the doctrine of Jesus Christ and the Gospel, would become soaked in indigenous cultural elements. Much to their regret, unable to travel and preach personally in all the dispersed communities, they had to rely on indigenous catechists to try to indoctrinate them, and they couldn't watch the exact transmission of the Christian message that, on translating it to the diverse autochthonous languages and exposing it to the varying religious conceptions of the different aboriginal groups, it suffered, irremediably, profound transformations. The tarahumara never assimilated Christianity in its pure form, for it was a religion of unknown concepts and values, foreign to their idiosyncrasy. Forced to accept Christianity, they modified it, adapting it to their beliefs. In the end, the church had to tolerate the inclusion of pagan practices and rites in order to penetrate partially in the indigenous culture.

At about 1631, important deposits of silver were discovered in Parral, attracting a multitude of fortune seekers and mine workers, followed by Spanish farmers and graziers who, to provide food to the mining zone, appropriated by force the best agricultural terrains, adjacent to rivers and streams, despoiling the tarahumaras not only of their lands but also of the water necessary for irrigation. Frequently the cattle of the Spaniards invaded the indigenous fields, destroying their crops and competing against their small herds, which were just being formed.

So much arbitrariness compelled many rarámuris to enter the most inaccessible places of the sierra, displacing other aboriginal groups established there. Since time immemorial, all these indigenous people had shared life with one another, trading, uniting by matrimony and, at times, waging war, though, due to the similitude of their way of life, the alterations suffered were minimum and easily assimilated. The arrival of the Spaniards occasioned a complex interaction of cultures extremely opposed. Cornered in the most recondite areas of the canyons, many tribes disappeared gradually, by extermination or by fusion with the new inhabitants, adopting their system of life, relegating their customs and denying their origin. To this aggregated the constant epidemics that decimated the indigenous communities. Some ethnic groups like the Témoris, the Chínipas, the Guazapares, and the forgotten Tubares, became extinct before being able to know their culture.

Initially the Tarahumara was part of the mission of the Tepehuanes, which to a great measure was in the care of the Franciscans. Because of the existence of a different language in the region and on advancing the colonization, extending the territory it comprised, arose the need of forming a new missionary unit. In 1639 the Tarahumara mission was created remaining in the hands of the Jesuits. The first established section, denominated Low Tarahumara or Ancient Tarahumara, encompassed a broad strip of land between Parral and the present city of Chihuahua. About thirty five years later, due to the displacement of the Indians toward the Sierra Madre Occidental, a second section more extensive was founded, contiguous and to the northwest from the preceding, receiving the name of High Tarahumara or New Tarahumara. In time this terminology was modified because of the migration of the tarahumaras toward the southwest, to the most rugged areas of the sierra. At present, the zone of the plateaus and the mountainous peaks is referred as High Tarahumara, and Low Tarahumara to the profundities of the canyons. The large central plains of the state have been occupied by the mestizos.

Curiously, in spite of the numerous local chronicles, there are no verifiable data of the origin of the name *"tarahumara"*; since their first narrations, the missionaries used this term, or variations of the same such as *"taraomare"* and *"tarumari."* Before the XIX century there is no single reference to the name *"rarámuri,"* which these Indians call themselves. It has been speculated that the Spaniards took the expression, already deformed, from the tepehuanes, neighbors of the tarahumaras, with which they had contact in the first place; in time and the accent of the peninsular pronunciation the word *"rarámuri"* would have derived in the current *"tarahumara."* Nowadays, the Indians use *"rarámuri"* when they speak among themselves in their language, and *"tarahumara,"* or its variants, when conversing in Spanish with the mestizos. It has been intended to give multiple meanings to the term *"rarámuri,"* for instance: *"swift foot,"* relating it to the enormous capacity of the tarahumara to run; but there has not been any general agreement. When I asked a rarámuri teacher the question, he answered flatly criticizing the *"whites"*: *"those are things of the "chabochis," to us it is only a name; the way in which we call ourselves."*

The contact with the Spaniards generated important changes in the technological field, the political organization and the religious order. Some cultural contributions were accepted willingly, like the metal axe, that permitted a better utilization of the resources of the forest; the plow, which facilitated the cultivation labors; and the introduction of domestic animals: hens, sheep, goats, cows, mules and horses, whose products, such as meat, provided a source of food more stable than hunting. They learned to make cheese, and wool soon substituted the vegetal fibers in the making of clothing. Manure, as fertilizer, maintained the quality of the lands of cultivation. These innovations occasioned changes in the distribution of family work: the tending of livestock devolved upon the women and the children as it adapted to their activities of firewood and wild fruit gathering; for hunting and agriculture, which were the occupations of the men, it was hindering. The possession of herds consolidated the habits of seasonal migration that, in the precolonial epoch, only occurred in the regions near to the canyons. To protect the animals from the harsh winter of the sierras it was necessary to move them into the more benign climate of the canyons.

Possibly at the beginning of our century the huarache with tire rubber sole and tied to the foot with leather straps was introduced, which, for its lightness and resistance, turned out the ideal complement for the long walks of the rarámuri; substituting the little durable traditional footwear, made all of untanned pelt, which was used with the hair inward to pad it. At present, the use of machetes, hoes, knives, lighters, metallic corn mills, needles and synthetic cloths is common.

The political organization was also modified on creating new systems of command. The ancient indigenous structures of government were very simple; occasionally, little chiefs appeared who led their community during some conflict, but they had a rather limited authority. The missionaries appointed indigenous officials to administer the missionary centers and as representatives of the tarahumaras in their dealings with the Spanish authority. Thus, the rarámuri governors and their retinue of assistants originated, establishing an elaborate command structure with well delimited jurisdictions. Nowadays, the names that receive the rarámuri officials reveal clearly their Spanish origin: alawasi for alguacil (sheriff), alacante for alcalde, sontárasi for soldado (soldier), mayoli for mayor and capitane for capitán (captain), among other positions. The duties of these rulers augmented gradually, delegating to them the responsibility of punishing the indigenous delinquents to prevent the resentment of the Indians against the missionaries. Still not long ago minor infractions such as theft were punished by lashing in public, until the Mexican government terminated that custom. Basically, the structures of self-government established in the Colony have been preserved till now.

It is indisputable that the teachings of the missionaries influenced the rarámuri religion and cosmovision. Although in some aspects these repercussions were more of form than of depth, and they took only the concepts that strengthened their beliefs and way of life, in others they produced an extraordinary syncretism, amalgamating perfectly both cultures. Today it is hard to discern which components are authentically indigenous. Their deities incarnated in the catholic divinities, recognizing the Christian god to their own God Father, linked to the sun, and the Virgin Mary to their Goddess Mother, associated with the moon. This transfiguration went farther on; the Most Holy Trinity and the notion of the redemption of man by virtue of the crucifixion of Jesus Christ are absent, and neither confession nor penance is performed. Almost a century after initiating their pastoral labor, the missionaries complained of not being able to administer the sacrament of the Eucharist to the Indians, because they were *"incapable of understanding the idea of God hidden in the Host."* On the other hand, dancing was their manner of praying or giving thanks, and it was not difficult to impose them the catholic festive calendar with its rituals such as the celebration of Holy Week and the dances of the Matachines.

Most likely, since the beginning of their evangelizing labor, the missionaries instituted the sermons that the siríames or indigenous governors pronounce before their community, in the parvis of the churches, after finishing the religious services, as part of the mechanism to facilitate the teaching of the Christian doctrine. These sermons have the purpose of advising and reiterating norms of conduct that favor sharing life socially, and help the partial transmission of the indigenous conception of the universal order, besides establishing the relation and obligations of the rarámuris with their deities. With their extensive knowledge of the autochthonous language, the religious had to translate the Christian concepts into rarámuri terms, including admonitions of social and individual behavior. No doubt they censored their public expression to ratify their contents and ensure that the information transmitted was in accordance with the ideology and the Christian moral values that they tried to inculcate. Nevertheless, as the time went by and on diminishing the meddling of the missionaries on the life of the tarahumaras, the sermons acquired little by little a larger number of aboriginal elements, until arriving to the current versions in which the Christian ideas fuse completely with the indigenous beliefs.

Many tarahumaras accepted living in the missions, but the system didn't work as expected; before reaching half a century from its formation, the Indians began to desert from the towns. Several factors occasioned this failure: the scarce labor force in the immense territories of the north of the Colony and the difficulty to get it from heathen Indians from the sierras, who resisted violently, compelled the Spaniards to resort to the missions to get workers for the mines and the agricultural fields; frequently they performed forced recruiting of Indians in the towns. Many rarámuris suffered from slavery and had to bear ill-treatment not only from the Spanish colonists

but also from the missionaries themselves who, when the Indians didn't follow the established rules of conduct and morality, punished them by lashing.

In many missions the lands of cultivation assigned to them were insufficient to support the indigenous population concentrated in them. Besides, compelled to simultaneously care for the Spanish cultivations, the Indians neglected their own crops, diminishing their production and suffering from hunger because of the scarcity of food. To this added the incursions of rival Indians like the tobosos, the cabezas and the salineros, from the region of the Bolsón de Mapimí, who plundered the missions and murdered their defenseless inhabitants.

The Spaniards brought to America diseases unknown to the Indians, for which they had not developed immunity because, living in an isolated continent, they never had been in contact with those microbes. The consequences of the contagion were terrible; unarmed before the viruses of smallpox, measles and other European diseases, grave epidemics broke out decimating the aboriginal population of the New World. The narrations of the horrible mortality are frightful; heaps of corpses of children and adults, covered with bloody pocks, were incinerated in enormous bonfires. In the Tarahumara, the Indians of the missions, living crowded and in continuous contact with the Spaniards, suffered from frequent and severe epidemics that caused a dreadful loss of lives. The heathen Indians, who lived dispersed in the mountains and far from the colonists, were little affected by the infections. Very consternated, the rarámuris soon associated the living in the missions with exposing themselves to contract the mortal diseases brought about by the invaders; so many calamities, born from their relationship with them, occasioned the indigenous disbandment from the missionary centers.

Compared to other neighboring autochthonous groups, the tarahumaras were of a peaceable nature. They resisted pacifically the oppression and renouncing of their culture by fleeing to inhospitable places to avoid encounter with the Spaniards, or they accepted living in the missions simulating submitting to their authority and religion; on not succeeding in moderating the vexations they suffered, they revolted violently. In the initial period of the colonization there were several uprisings, some of large magnitude in which thousands of warriors participated. As a rule, these uprisings began with the insurrection of the inhabitants of a mission, who murdered the missionaries, destroyed the church, and afterwards attacked the haciendas of the Spanish settlers. Nevertheless, the consequences of these revolts resulted more adverse for the Indians themselves; they were crushed militarily with the help of Christianized Indians, who formed the main body of the armies, and gave a pretext for the conquistadores to carry out slaughters, enslave more tarahumaras and raze their properties. Many towns were relocated, separating numerous families.

In the XVIII century the rarámuris often united to the apaches to make forays against the Spanish possessions. This alliance was much feared because the rarámuris, who were experts in their territory, guided the apaches to make dexterous attacks to the richest colonies, then vanishing in the sierra. At the end of the XIX century, after the army of the United States defeated the apaches of the chiricagua tribe, the relationship between the two indigenous groups changed radically, emerging a ferocious rivalry. Bands of apaches attacked the rarámuri communities perpetrating atrocities, while the tarahumaras served in the Mexican army, helping to track and combat them. It is said that two rarámuris killed Victorio, the combative apache chief, in 1880. In this period, the apaches domineered the north of Chihuahua and Sonora, and their devastating incursions arrived as far as Durango. For their bellicosity, slyness and resistance they were very difficult to combat, and their sudden attacks kept the settlers of the haciendas and towns of the region appalled. It was then when the popular phrase *"Alas Chihuahua, what a lot of apaches!"* appeared. The problem was so grave that the governor of the state offered rewards for their heads, but a short time later he had to revoke the order because the mestizos, to earn money, killed pacific tarahumaras, tearing them off the scalp and the skin of the face, presenting them as apaches for, thus, differentiating them was highly complicated. In later epochs the rarámuri resistance against the colonization was more and more sporadic and limited; although it is told that, at dates as recent as 1969, there was an intent of rebellion in a remote corner of the sierra.

In 1767, accused, among other things, of utilizing the missions to become rich and get political power, the Jesuits were expelled from all the Spanish possessions in the world. The news left many civilians stunned, who protested indignantly, considering it a dirty calumny of the Borbones kings, but they were harshly repressed. That year, hundreds of heartbroken Jesuits traveled, in little groups, the arduous roads of the Colony; on foot or on litters they headed for México City to continue toward the port of Veracruz, following which then was considered as the most traveled road of America. An ancient anecdote narrates that, as the religious were passing by Jalapa, the poorest muleteers of the place, defying the authority, felt pity for their lamentable condition and, offering them their mules and horses, carried them as far as the coast. Riding without harnesses, the disheartened missionaries seemed quixotic personages no longer in favor. Only the oldest ones and the sick, who were unable to continue the long journey toward exile, were allowed to stay, confining them in convents. Their evangelizing labor was interrupted completely and their properties were confiscated, affecting the Indians who depended on them.

Franciscans took charge of the Tarahumara, but for lack of resources they didn't succeed in continuing the work of the Jesuits and the mission was neglected. Forsaken, the tarahumaras abandoned the missionary centers returning to their ancient home, though incorporating the contributions legated by the Jesuits. The cultural pattern that arose on integrating the teachings of the missionaries into the rarámuri life, was consolidated about the middle of the XVIII century and has long lasted until this day. Little by little, the system of *"reduction"* was eliminated as impractical. With the return of the tarahumaras to their dispersed hamlets, the missions were transformed into ceremonial centers where the indigenous population only assembles to celebrate their religious festivities or to resolve commercial and political matters. On returning to the sierras, the rarámuris who lived in the missions spread the new culture all over the region, influencing the heathen Indians, who received it already synthesized. The religious lamented that the Indians fled from the towns, said masses, celebrated matrimonies and baptized, imitating the sacraments of the church, conceding them the same validity than to those administered by clergymen. At the present time, in many remote communities the religious ceremonies are performed without the presence of priests, and there is, even, reluctance to accept them.

In 1821, with the triumph of the insurgents and the birth of the independent México, the Spanish missionaries were expelled from the country and the possessions of the church were reduced considerably, worsening the situation of the missions. With the Reform of Benito Juárez, in 1859, the religious orders were suppressed in México, nationalizing their properties. These events liberated the Indians from the domination of the missionary centers, favoring their self-determination, and they were one of the main factors that allowed them to preserve their ancestral cultural traits.

In 1900 the return of the Jesuits to México was authorized, but they only returned to the Tarahumara, trying to reestablish their ancient system of missions. The Revolution of 1910 hindered again their labor because the state of Chihuahua was the scene of important bellicose episodes and, besides, all the foreign Jesuits were deported to the United States by General Francisco Villa. At the end of the decade of the 1920's, during the anticlericalism of President Calles, their activities also were made difficult. Nowadays, the Jesuits have concentrated their efforts in a small group of missions and have changed their evangelizing strategy, giving priority to the rendering of social services like the construction of schools, workshops and hospitals; relegating their religious mission to a secondary goal, they have attained good acceptance and respect from the Indians. Nevertheless, there is no lack of religious who pretend to assume hegemonic attitudes toward the tarahumaras, longing for the old times of the all-powerful church.

At the arrival of the Spaniards, the Tarahumara was extremely rich in natural resources; the forests extended as far as the plains and the fauna was very abundant. The natives had preserved them as part of their culture, which inculcated the respect for nature. According to the chronicles of the first missionaries, they were animists and believed that all living beings had a soul and should be treated with great deference. They did not consider the animals inferior; on the contrary, they tried to learn from them. They thought they knew vital secrets like predicting snowfalls. According to tradition, the animals taught them to dance; thus, in their dances propitiatory of rain they imitated the movements of the deer. An ancestral myth warned them of being good to the animals or, at the end of the world, they would take revenge on those who would have treated them with cruelty, finishing them in the same way; for that reason, they asked permission of their

spirits to kill only what was necessary to subsist, keeping some of their parts in order to acquire their qualities. They feared certain animals, like the coyote and the owl, relating them to the sorcerers who could cause them harm.

They rendered cult to idols that represented the natural spirits and forces, like the wind or the lightning, dedicating offerings and ceremonies that lasted whole days, invoking their goodwill to provide them with sustenance, improving the fertility of the fields, or cure diseases. Even at present, one of the functions of the healers is to communicate with the gods to solicit or thank for favors. In their sermons, the indigenous governors proclaim the responsibility the tarahumaras have of taking care of the world by divine command. This mentality, that today we would call ecological, is a common characteristic of all the autochthonous cultures of America.

With the arrival of the white man, in a short time the equilibrium maintained by millenniums was disturbed. Enormous expanses of forest were razed to provide dwellings, fuel, fences and cultivation fields to a population in sudden and excessive growth. Firearms and immoderate hunting caused the extinction of many animal species; others took refuge in inaccessible places, more and more scarce. Of the large mammals of the Sierra Madre the only remains are their furs adorning some homes, as opprobrious proofs of the massacre. The introduction of domestic livestock, foreign to the environment, had a persistent negative impact on the ecosystem, the most destructive being the porcine, which is raised free and is very noxious for the natural vegetation. As if that were not enough, the inadequate exploitation of the mines occasioned the pollution of the rivers with chemical toxic residues.

At the end of the XIX century, a railroad was built to simplify the transport of wood and minerals out of the sierra, facilitating the access to depredators. In this epoch, deforestation reached frightful levels; after finishing the forests in the United States, numerous North American companies, concealed by the government of Porfirio Diaz, looted with impunity the wood of the country. Only the outbreak of the Mexican Revolution impeded the total destruction of the chihuahuan forests. Nowadays, although to a minor scale than in times of yore, the irrational felling of trees, whose trunks, piled up as tragic skeletons, decay in vain in the open air, still persists. Recently, a road circuit that crosses part of the sierra was completed, favoring the entrance of new settlers and accelerating a dramatic change in the way of life of its inhabitants. Encircled by civilization and with no other place to escape, as in former times, the tarahumaras face a desperate struggle to preserve their culture.

He liked to be called *"Manuelón,"* and always proudly showed a couple of books about mining, in English, in which his name was *"written in large letters"*; he did not understand what they said but someone had translated them to him, they recommended him as an excellent guide for anyone who would be interested in exploiting the mines of the place, *"if you need any information look for him in his little shoppe, by the river."* The *"little shoppe"* was an ancient large warehouse made of adobe with a very high ceiling, just the same as all the old large houses of the village. On the rough and enormous shelves of coarse wood, almost empty, the dust accumulated and spiders languished, waiting for the improbable arrival of a fly that would get entangled in the mortal symmetry of their cobwebs. Rusted mining tools hung from the walls evoking old times. The place seemed to live only of the handful of memories that Manuelón recounted without cease to those who would want to devote a moment to listen to him. Then, moved with emotion, he seemed to absent himself; behind his thick eyeglasses, which shrank his eyes as if they had sunk down to the middle of his skull, his look ran away, wandering through the canyons in search of a fantastic chink that would concede it to penetrate into a secret subterranean hideout, where the past would be sheltered.

He had devoted his entire life to mining and was a great expert in techniques of exploitation on a small scale. With pleasure he remembered those cool dawns of his youth when, accompanied by a select group of friends, they left the village protected by the darkness so that nobody would know where they went, so that nobody would discover their precious veins. On mule back they carried shovels, pickaxes, hoes, provisions; ascending the arduous slopes for hours as far as the black narrow entrance of the mines. There they spent days, scratching the entrails of the earth by the withered light of the carbide lamps; helpless in the depth of the treacherous galleries that snatched the lives of many of their comrades. Then, the return followed, carrying the heavy sacks of ore that made the robust beasts of burden snort, and the laborious process of pulling out the coveted metals from the rocks; there came into action the *"taunas,"* primitive and ingenious hydraulic turbines, utilized in grinding, which profit from the force of the water from the rivers, carried by narrow channels, to revolve a wheel with wooden blades which drags two large blocks of quarry stone inside a circular deposit filled with water and fragments of ore, to triturate them until converting them into mud. Lastly they added to the mixture the quicksilver to amalgamate the gold and the silver, and fuse them into diminutive ingots. All ran the risk of ending their lives suffering from the incapacitating tremor that, mysteriously, affected many miners, who earned the depreciatory nickname of *"quicksilvered"* when medical science discovered that it was caused by a serious mercurial intoxication.

But it was a long time since Manuelón had worked in the mines; the accessible veins had been exhausted and it was necessary to use more potent and efficacious methods to find new deposits. However, the sale and use of explosives had been prohibited, and the army performed a most rigorous labor of vigilance. At first they said it was to prevent accidents for, until a short time ago, some mestizos of the canyon towns used dynamite cartridges as a not at all orthodox method of fishing, throwing them into the ponds formed on the margins of the rivers; in spite of the spectacularity of the technique, it was not efficient and the majority of the fish ended up torn asunder. Still one meets people with hands or arms mutilated as a result of those extravagant practices. As months elapsed, control measures grew stricter; *"they are very fierce,"* said Manuelón, worried, *"they fear it might fall in the hands of drug smugglers, or, as you see, what is happening with the guerrilla"*; with frustration he lamented, *"those who pay the consequences are the honest people; they don't let us work and so here we are, all busted."*

Mining was the main promoter of the colonization of the Nueva España; sixty years after the fall of Tenochtitlán a good part of its territory had been already occupied due to the explorations in order to find gold and silver. Although by decree the mines belonged to the king, a complicated legislation was established to grant rights of exploitation in exchange of the payment of one fifth of the profit to the Spanish Crown. In every Real de Minas (mining town) a royal till existed in charge of collecting the famous *"royal fifth"* before sealing the ingots of precious metals that were extracted in every site. In spite of it, the extraordinary riches of the mines created opulent cities whose inhabitants swelled with conceit in ostentation and squandering. Nevertheless, the rudimentary techniques available only permitted the exploitation of sites where ores were superficial and almost pure; on exhausting these veins a severe economic depression supervened, sinking into poverty many Reales de Minas, which were deserted and condemned to oblivion.

As in other regions of the republic, some towns of the tarahumara sierra arose in the proximities of the mining centers. The discovery of a vein attracted hordes of adventurers, traders and service providers who, all of a sudden, established a new community. At the peak of their highest grandeur, several villages of the canyons grew to have thousands of inhabitants. Magnificentvestiges of the splendor of that epoch are still conserved, like the ruins of the sumptuous mansions of the proprietors of the mines, and it's easy to go astray in the intricate galleries of the ancient mines, in the imposing sepulchral silence of which, the shrill resounding of footsteps seems a fugitive echo from the past that were trapped in the startling blackness of the tunnels. There is no shortage here of stories of specters who haunt at night amongst the dilapidated walls, longing for the lost glory, or of unfortunate ghosts of beheaded miners who pitifully suffer purgation in the interior of the mines.

Luckily, in these sierras, minerals are found dispersed in small lodes, what has hindered the establishment of large mining companies as their exploitation is profitable only for the free-lance gold diggers of the neighboring villages, whose investment is minimum. Nonetheless, recently, on the boundary with the state of Sinaloa, a North American company discovered a huge deposit of gold, building an impressive industrial complex requiring transport of machinery hanging from helicopters through the canyons. The construction of the plant and the development of operations have gnawed the neighboring hills, destroying the vegetation, shaping an earthy clearing in the greenness of the mountains that, from afar, stands out like a mangy bald spot on the wrinkled skin of the planet.

Thirty dogs fought furiously in the middle of the town's main street, raising a dense cloud of dust that hid them and, in the weak luminosity of dusk, barely allowed distinguishing them as vague silhouettes throwing ferocious bites all around them. It all began with the coquettish debauch of a female dog in rut that crossed carelessly the bystreets of the town, congregating a multitude of males that followed her tenaciously. Amidst failed tries to win her favors animosity heated up, and it sufficed a simple shove for unchaining that violent vortex of frightful growls, pitiless bites and heartrending howls. The bloody fight of all against all disturbed the residents of the neighboring houses, frightening the children, who hid behind the doors and windows. Unexpectedly the rumbling of a motor was heard and a minute later the town was filled with light, pulling a sounding expression of joy from its inhabitants and disconcerting the herd of dogs that, fearfully, stopped fighting and disbanded running.

On returning peace, Don Rosendo, who had observed the battle from the sidewalk, went back to his shop grumbling against commotion and electricity. A short time ago the electric company had put to work a powerhouse, and though it only ran some four hours at dusk, the novelty induced many to buy electric household appliances to use them *"while the light lasts."* Problems started when parts, fuel and maintenance of the machines had to be paid; soon inopportune blackouts began due to failures. That was why Don Rosendo preferred his gas refrigerator; *"they just tell you nice things to persuade you"* he said, choleric. But what unhinged him the most was television; soap operas monopolized the attention of housewives, and some caused such a furor that flatly paralyzed the activities in all the town. Even worse was the influence on children; it attracted them like a magnet and *"they remained glued"* to it, neglecting their school and household chores, *"dulling them"* with the unlikely feats of a bunch of *"effeminate and bragging"* heroes who paled next to the discreet fortitude of the sierra cowboys, accustomed to sleep in the country after exhausting horseback rides to go perform their daily hard tasks. The arrival of his

grandson interrupted his reasoning; clenching firmly in the hands he brought several little metal balls that, as he put them on the counter, emitted beautiful golden sparkles; his father had sent him to weigh them. They were the product of his last day's work in a rich vein of gold he recently had discovered, and whose location he zealously kept secret.

That night there was a grand *"fiesta"*; the central square of the town appeared very lively bound with multicolored light bulbs, and the clamor of loudspeakers incited couples to dance to the rhythm of the cumbias, the corriditas and the ranchero polkas. Programmed to end by midnight, it was prolonged till dawn because many *"enfiestados,"* euphoric by the alcohol, decided to cooperate to *"throw"* more gasoline to the power station. The collection was so successful that it was sufficient to hire a local musical group, which, on contagion of the popular rejoicing, made them a spectacular rebate. For two hours the vocalist, half drunk, reeled on an improvised stage, uttering disorderly shouts the discordant audience choired, trying just barely to follow the time of the guitar, the accordion and the contrabass. Only God knows how many maledictions they received from those who were trying to get some sleep.

The next afternoon I went to stroll by the riverside; the roar of the torrent descending through some rocky rapids effaced the monotonous squeaking of the taunas incessantly revolving in the borders. In one of them grinding had finished; Don Rosendo helped his son gathering the tools, and just as I approached they opened the sluice of the deposit, draining to the water the mineral surplus mixed with residues of toxic chemicals. A thick greenish brown stain formed on the surface, flowing downstream carried by the current; little by little it penetrated to the bottom, expanding until reaching the two borders. As a repugnant monster it advanced, inexorable, poisoning fish and polluting the earth. Minutes later it encompassed all the riverbed; now nothing would impede it to arrive to the sea.

1012
C H P

Even in the middle of the fields the clangor was deafening, and on entering the obscurity of the tunnels it became hallucinating; the walls repeated it without cease in tangled echoes disarranging reality. The violent agitation, the vibration of the engine under the feet, the shrill creaking of the wheels on the rails, the precipitate flight from the profundities of the earth, illuminated by the flashing passing of the headlight, provoked vertigo… The world seemed about to explode. Such a chaotic disorder was impossible to comprehend with the intellect, which grasped the dazzling beam of light to escape from the confusion of darkness. When the whistle liberated its monstrous and tearing roar that turned maddening. From the bottom of my soul I only happened to ask myself: *How have men been able to invent, to arrive at this terrible insanity?*

It all began when the engineer saw me struggling to take a photo and invited me to see the driver's cab. The narrow compartment was filled with gauges, levers and greasy instruments. In the unhinging din we talked loudly. Minutely, he explained his work routine: crews were relieved midway, passing the night there in old railroad cars adapted as lodging, to wait the following day for the train coming from the coast and drive it back to Chihuahua. They spent the nights playing cards, and in the mornings they went to run through the forest. Very proud he said that nothing stopped the railroad… *"Well, unless there would be a large landslide blocking the tracks; but neither rain nor snow stop it."* At times, loud detonations were heard, and the engineer, making a droll and exaggerated expression of alarm, exclaimed jokingly: *"it got a flat!"* They were petards used as warning signs which exploded on passing the locomotive. When I told him I was looking for a spectacular photo of the railroad, he took me to sit on the front of the engine, holding on to the protection railing, and there I stayed, feeling the frigid wind hitting me in the face, till the light of the evening vanished.

The railroad arrived for the first time to the sierra tarahumara on the last part of the XIX century. It was built, in the beginning, by North Americans to facilitate the transport of wood and minerals their companies extracted unrestrictedly from the chihuahuan sierras, leaning on the porfirista politics that allowed the looting of the country for the sake of a supposed progress and technological advance, from which only foreigners and an elite of millionaires in power profited. Shortly after, based on these privileges and disposing of the Mexican territory as if it were their property, they conceived an ambitious project to establish a shorter commercial route connecting the central region of the United States with a port of the Pacific, and to be able to export their agricultural and industrial production to the rest of America and the Asiatic countries. Fortunately, the Mexican Revolution frustrated these purposes on overthrowing Porfirio Diaz and halting the opprobrious rapine. The plan to open a new way to the sea was abandoned. During many years, this railroad line kept the original name of Kansas City, México y Oriente, reaching only the boundaries of the Sierra Madre Occidental.

The unbelievable ruggedness of the region, which makes communication extremely difficult, has been the main factor that has maintained isolated the area inhabited by the tarahumaras, who, without problem, have always moved on foot through the canyons and mountains. With the introduction of donkeys and mules, upon the arrival of the Spaniards, muleteers and their droves became the principal means to transport loads along the royal roads that connected the ancient haciendas and towns. The oldest inhabitants of the towns of the canyons still remember how, just some decades ago, it took them almost twenty days to go with their burros to trade merchandise in the limits of the sierra.

In 1961, after arduous and costly work, performed exclusively by Mexicans, the ancient project of joining the central plains of Chihuahua with the coast of the Pacific could finally be accomplished. Inaugurated under the name of Chihuahua-Pacífico or CH-P, as it is popularly known, this railroad line constitutes a monumental work of modern engineering; tearing off hills, removing tons of stones, blowing up rocks to bore the earth, thirty five bridges and eighty six tunnels were built, the longest of almost two kilometers, to cross rivers and mountains, in a fascinating and exotic course across immense semiarid plains, high plateaus covered with temperate forests and profound canyons tapestried with exuberant tropical jungles. Such a daring effort, in the heart of a landscape so strange and enchanting, has inspired the imagination of writers and script makers. To show pride for the power of the railroad to conquer abysses and water currents, besides advertising to attract tourism, the train used the image of a tarahumara runner as a symbol. Ironically, the advent of the railroad and its transporting capability favored the colonization of the region, causing drastic transformations that have contributed to the deterioration of the conditions of life of the aborigines.

The railway crosses the Tarahumara leaving a rosary of stations which have consolidated into population centers, acquiring great commercial importance; from them depart numerous dirt roads that have invaded the most remote corners of the region. Furniture, provisions, tools, materials and all kind of merchandise go into the sierra through the railroad that, from its inauguration, has had a capital importance for the mestizos, originating a critical dependency and vulnerability of their economy because, if the train is delayed or stops running or when, for absurd regulations, freight transport is limited, it arises a severe crisis of supplies in the sierra, raising prices. Although there exists an ancient dirt road with a path similar to that of the tracks, and follows them for a good part of their course, its bad conditions impede its commercial use.

There is a singular atmosphere in the sierra towns; an air of the Old West, a vague flavor of rough frontier; as if they were the entrance to an untamed and primitive world, a doorway to the México Bronco. It is captivating to see their wooden houses with pitched roofs, their smoky chimneys filling the air with a pleasant aroma of burned resin, their sturdy cowboys riding by the dusty and sloped streets; their nights illuminated by oil lamps reminding bygone epochs, and the variegated crowd that congregates in the station on the arrival of the train, announced by its piercing whistles which rouse the lethargic little towns. Unfortunately, it is this charm that has attracted one of the most noxious plagues of our time: tourism. Unlike the obstinate travelers of yore who endured discomforts and penuries in their long journeys to know remote places and exotic cultures in their natural state, the modern tourist imposes conditions and demands comforts to *"favor"* a place with his presence. From his myopic perspective, he is the important one, not the site he visits. Clear example would be the attitude of two German young women who, after spending several days in the towns of the canyons, came out annoyed, complaining of having gotten exhausted because they had not found more than tortillas and beans to eat, suspecting the people denied them food. Unaware of reality, they didn't conceive that was all the miserable inhabitants of the villages had to eat. It's, also, revealing the case of a North American tourist who, fed up with eating the local dishes, he complained angrily against the owners of the restaurants for not having *"real food; a good hamburger with fries."*

More and more hotel and service companies are created to offer all kinds of facilities to the tourists, so they can enjoy *"the magic of the Tarahumara."* On the supposed purpose of supporting the economy and bringing progress to the chihuahuan sierra, the construction of a huge tourist complex has been programmed, beginning with the paving of roads to improve the routes of access. The official reports already proclaim the juicy gainings that will be obtained. Unfortunately, those who benefit from these concessions and monopolize the generated riches are the large investors coming from outside the sierra and without any roots in it. The Tarahumara only receives the garbage and the negative impact of such projects. Few are the tourists who come with full consciousness of the fragile ecological balance of the region, and how significant the existence of human groups that grasp to the earth, struggling to keep their ancestral way of life, is. In their short stay, most of the visitors don't manage to notice that their presence furthers the disappearance of the indigenous culture and the pollution and destruction of the landscape, whose pristine beauty and quietude motivated their visit.

At first, the railroad was simply a means of communication and transport for the towns of the sierra; with the increase of tourism, its function was modified to take advantage of it. Of its two daily runs, the first class one was devoted, in fact, to serve tourists. Equipped with the best cars and, in its good, old days, with elegant stewards and dining car, it only stops in a limited number of stations that give access to tourist centers, making a pretty efficient course. In the high season of tourism, when demand is larger, the admission to the train is very reserved and in extreme cases it acquires racist tints. Priority is given to groups of foreign tourists who make multitudinous reservations and boarding is impeded to the inhabitants of the sierra, to whom the train services have a primordial importance, not a superfluous function. Sometimes the train doesn't even stop in the station, leaving in a lurch the wrathful crowd that, after the long waiting, can only see it passing by. Even if he had the money to buy a ticket, a tarahumara wouldn't be allowed to travel in this train; a dirty and malodorous Indian is not something that helps to promote tourism.

The second class train is destined for *"la raza"*; in it travel the people of meager resources. Since it stops at all the small villages along the route, its course is prolonged interminably, arriving to its destination until the wee hours of the morning. Its slowness is proverbial and gives the impression that running one would arrive sooner. In its deteriorated cars passengers throng to excess, sharing the space with hens, turkeys, goats and even pigs, which some people transport in the crammed luggage compartments. On spreading the fame that the first class train was full of wealthy tourists, assaults began. On the way out from the sierra toward the coast, in a secluded spot of narrow canyons covered with abundant thicket, region renowned for its violent people engaged in the cultivation of drugs, gangs of bandits with the face covered, riding horses and armed with *"goat's horns,"* assaulted the train boarding it in the purest Wild West style, helped by accomplices who, traveling incognito in the train, on arriving at a predetermined place they forced the crew to stop it. The frequency of the attacks and the gravity of the atrocities perpetrated increased to the point of provoking international alarm when several foreign tourists were injured and, some, killed during the assaults. The protection with escorts of policemen and even soldiers heavily armed became necessary. It is told that on one occasion they tried to rob the second class train, but the surprised were the assailants because the passengers, brave people of village accustomed to carry weapons, repelled the aggression. In the shooting, several malefactors died and the rest took flight frightened by the unexpected counterattack. Apparently, due to the greater risk and the possibility of a less promising booty, the second class train didn't suffer assaults again. In recent times, the economic situation of this railroad line has deteriorated much; to the preceding problems added a bad and corrupt administration and a worst utilization of resources. Before the prospect of an imminent bankruptcy, its privatization was considered appropriate.

The aborigines who live in the zones near the railroad have also learned to profit from tourism, establishing small stalls of handcrafts in the stations. However, competition is fierce and even unfair. A large quantity of merchants, many of them come from the outside, have formed true street markets beside the tarahumaras, selling manufactures and products brought in from other states. The local mestizos have designed their own handcrafts imitating the rarámuris or, taking advantage of their attraction, they elaborate rag dolls decked out like tarahumaras. To be able to stand out in the market, the Indians constantly contrive new handcrafts they didn't produce before, originating a wide and complex variety of articles destined to satisfy the imagination and tastes of the tourists. At times some traders of the tourist centers buy their production in bulk at derisive prices, to resell it very dearly. Moreover, there are cases the merchant suggests innovations in the handcrafts to make them more saleable. Numerous tarahumaras have flatly devoted themselves to commerce and spend all day sitting by their stalls, elaborating baskets and figures. Many of them have abandoned the cultivation of their lands and the raising of cattle, and have even renounced their long walks through the sierra.

Unluckily, this change doesn't seem superficial. Manipulated by civilization, their lives and minds are gradually transforming, adapting to consumerism. Even their religious ceremonies have been commercialized, and in some places they charge a fee to allow entrance to visitors, resembling more and more publicity spectacles. Little by little, their mind and their soul have been trapped by the vertigo of modernism. The native is utilized to promote tourism, but as if he were a fanciful being. His idealized image must remain cloistered within the frame of a painting, neat and pure, frolicking in the midst of romantic bucolic scenes. His figure ought to further the legend and make tourists dream. The actual Indian and his misery, with all of his human defects and weaknesses, must be hidden, exterminated, so that he does not shame us, so that he does not destroy the charm of the sacred myth that ought to be adored at a distance. In the obtuse and prejudiced ideology of the modern world, the tarahumara who lives linked to the earth and to his millenary traditions, the real tarahumara, is something that opposes progress.

The dramatic accident occurred near the exit of a curved tunnel. An elderly man, former tarahumara governor, drove his three burros by the middle of the track loaded with sacks replete with leafy bundles of wild marjoram and laurel, which he had gathered in the fields during more than fifteen days. He was going toward the town to sell them. Two of his numerous grandchildren, both under ten years of age, accompanied him to help him because he was almost deaf and his sight was already failing; that was why he didn't notice that the train was approaching. The lunge was brutal; the donkeys were sent flying into the air all ripped apart, leaving a trail of viscera and blood.

XICO
FERROCA
6077
6090   PB

The mutilated body of the man was left unrecognizable, scrambled with the remains of the animals. The smashed packs went rolling a long stretch, scattering the load over the ground. Terrified, the engineer could do nothing to avoid running over them, they appeared suddenly on taking a turn in the tunnel; he only managed to operate the whistle which resounded causing shivers and making the entire obscure cavity tremble. Inexplicably neither the children reacted; they escaped *"by dint of a miracle"* when, in the last moment, they threw themselves into the deep ditches that limit the sides of the track. Weeks after the unfortunate occurrence, fragments of bones still remained stuck on the rails, and a heap of perfumed leaves, spread amongst the ties, swirled capriciously, agitated by the wind.

For three days we had been vaccinating children downstream, walking through the bottom of an immense canyon. It was the beginning of summer and the gorges had become a gigantic oven. All the time we wore our clothes soaked and sweat trickled abundantly down our foreheads. The heat was stifling, unnerving, maddening. Due to the drought, many streams had dried and the vegetation of the slopes had turned gray and yellow; rivers were only narrow rivulets that joined small ponds of crystalline water, resembling rosaries of iridescent beads. It was difficult to restrain the desire of having a dip all the time. Frequently, we went up and down steep trails or waded the river to go around the craggy hillsides and huge rocks that obstructed the way. The cold water and sharp stones of the riverbed made the crossings painful. At noon the mestizo villages of the riversides seemed deserted; their inhabitants stayed inside the houses to escape the fiery sun. Transformed into ghost towns, a dusty burning wind lashed constantly their forgotten narrow streets. In the afternoons the landscape appeared desolate and boredom reigned in the air; only, at times, the far beating of an indigenous drum disturbed the somnolent atmosphere, playing at a distance, hidden among the mountains.

Half-way through, we slept in one of the riparian settlements, in a house by the river. For lack of space, we had to take some cots out into the yard; in solidarity, the host also slept outside, warning us with dissimulated fear: *"let's see if the vampire does not fall on us."* It has been a very long time since the inhabitants of this region suffer attacks of vampires, but they considered them inoffensive; until some years ago, when *"the vampire fell"* on a girl and she died of rabies. The vision of that little child choking with the thick froth that stuffed up her mouth and nose, with the hands twitched and her eyes popping out of her head from terror on feeling life was escaping from her, left a deep impression in the residents of the place. Since then, when someone suffers a bite they take him immediately to the city to be vaccinated, a four-day journey, for it is difficult to find rabies vaccine in the small towns.

At nightfall of the following day we arrived at our destination, a settlement near the boundary with Sinaloa. In this zone there are no longer tarahumaras. Climate and vegetation are almost tropical and, for so propitious conditions, the cultivation of narcotics is common. It is an open secret though; for some people it is their only means of subsistence. Owing to that, the presence of army patrols in the area is constant. As soon as we got installed in a little cabin, two soldiers came to summon us to identify ourselves and to appear before the commander of a detachment encamped in the place. For a good while he shined his flashlight on our faces comparing them with our identification cards; satisfied, he let us leave, apologizing for the bother and justifying himself: *"hereabouts it is very dangerous and one must make sure they are friendly people."*

In the morning they went to visit us to the vaccination post. The commander was very young, I calculated he was younger than twenty five years of age; some of the soldiers looked like children, and even the uniform fitted them loose. I offered them candies and dried fruit. They had been in the zone a long time, and they were glad to be talking to outsiders, after being amongst so many villagers who regarded them as enemies. The health care officer requested our support with medication; several members had serious diarrheic problems and his medicine provision was almost exhausted; we also gave them analgesics, antibiotics and tablets against the endemic paludism. That was the first time they went to that locality and nobody knew the way; they guided themselves with a topographic map, but it didn't describe all the anfractuosities of the ravines; inevitably they had gone astray on several occasions. Each one carried more than thirty kilos between armament and provisions; for the one with the radio it was worse. They advanced always afraid of an ambush, and were worried about becoming exhausted to a degree of not being able to repel an attack. They told us about mafias that, in some parts, cheated or obliged peasants to sow narcotics and bought them, later, at ridiculous prices, threatening to denounce them if they did not accept it; dealing with aborigines they took advantage of them even more. They were fully aware of the difficult economic situation of those families and acknowledged: *"as long as they don't have another way of supporting themselves the problem is going to go on."*

Drug trafficking has become a terrible plague that spreads in an alarming way, affecting primordially the southern zone of the Tarahumara and the coastal watershed of the Sierra Madre Occidental, that is adjacent to the state of Sinaloa. This has propitiated a disagreeable atmosphere of tension in the region, exacerbated by the presence of the army and the police corporations that, sometimes, make the situation worse by committing abuses and arbitrary acts. In a little airport, right beside one of the main roads giving access to the sierra, a huge cargo airplane is now abandoned which for a long time made flights from South America, bringing large shipments of drugs. During months its furtive nocturnal landings, that the entire world knew, were kept in *"secret"*; until a discord between the criminals and the implicated authorities caused the illicit operation to be *"discovered and dismantled," "dealing contraband a hard blow."* Today, in sight of everybody, the deteriorated aircraft seems a shameful monument to corruption and dirty treacheries.

The exorbitant gainings of dirty money have allowed the acquisition of innumerable weapons, which have increased the violence in towns and villages. Few are the inhabitants of this zone who do not possess at least one, and it is common to meet presumptuous braggarts who intend to intimidate the others displaying sophisticated armaments, trying to compensate their inferiority

complexes and ignorance with the vain power of brute force and barbarity. When these attitudes are combined with the consumption of alcohol or drugs, the consequences are unpredictable. Shootings and murders caused by insignificant incidents like a slight involuntary damage in some property or a trifling traffic accident are not rare. Such is the insecurity that in certain places even women take arms with them, and attend balls carrying pistols. At times, the strife for the control of the market provokes atrocious vengeances between families, ending in true massacres. It is chilling to receive, in the hospitals of the area, children and women with limbs amputated or the abdomen rent and the viscera exposed, on being pitilessly injured with bursts of high power submachine guns. The employees of the governmental departments know well the fear of working in those places. The statistics of a teacher assigned to a rural school of the region for two years are revealing; only in that short period, eleven of his fellow teachers were murdered, in most cases by absurd motives like not having passed a pupil. Even a priest had been shot in the inside of his house through a window. *"Those people do not respect anybody,"* he said, alarmed, *"there, it sure is like in the Mexican song; life is worth nothing."*

Although, by now, the aborigines implicated in drug trafficking are few, their growing migration to the cities has exposed them to unknown problems. Taking advantage of their need, good faith and ignorance, groups of gangsters oblige tarahumara young men to sell drugs, besides inducing them in the vice to dominate them easily. In view of these facts, in governmental circles, worries have arisen that there are attempts to exploit on a large scale, the physical faculties of the rarámuri and his extraordinary knowledge of the sierra, to produce and traffic narcotics. They have been urged to give a definitive solution to the critical situation in which lives the aborigine, for the current conditions are propitious to compel him to seek new ways of survival, even if they are illegal, whose negative effects would be very hard to predict.

"Let's see if mice let you sleep," Rosendo cautioned me while I extended my sleeping bag on the floor, on some blankets he had lent me. *"They are very annoying; they spend all night making noise."* It was in the middle of darkness, looking for a cave or a flat space where to lie down, when I unexpectedly ran across the rustic hut of the tarahumara; all built with wooden boards, without windows, it was divided into two rooms: one, *"large,"* was used as bedroom, dining room and kitchen; in the other one, very small, there was a minuscule shop. Exhausted and benumbed by the intense cold, it was a pleasure to sit myself by the warmth of his improvised firewood stove made out of the half of a gasoline barrel. An oil lamp feebly illuminated the room creating a charming dreamlike atmosphere. This time I was not going to wake up in the midst of the frozen fields, all covered with ice; but I was going to miss the stars, which always stayed there staring at me until I closed my eyes.

I've just crossed one of the most uninhabited and remotest zones of the sierra; fifteen days mounting hills, descending into the profundities of the gorges, following occasionally narrow trails that soon disappeared in the thickness of the underbrush. I had waded rivers, breaking by kicks the thick layer of ice of the borders, arriving to the other side with the feet livid and numb. A whole day I had not met anybody, the only human trace was a rickety empty house, whose residents were surely begging in some city to survive the winter. A feeble dog *"guarded"* the scarce belongings piled up under a shed, and as I approached it fled aghast to hide in the thicket. Farther on, in the bottom of a narrow canyon, I found several cave paintings in red ochre color, adorning the foot of a monumental rock wall. Although the technique was very primitive, the motifs were modern: an automobile, an airplane, a cap with spectacles.

Now, in the silence of the night only the far-off beating of a drum was heard. *"They are having a tesgüinada,"* Rosendo warned me, *"they surely come to wake us up in the early morning to buy something"*; the gentility of his address and such an affable character amazed me. He was turning fifty. In his adolescence he had had the opportunity of studying with the Jesuits, *"they teach you a lot of things."* He hadn't drunk in a long time, *"it harms the body and the pocket,"* he said convinced. In his house there was an order and cleanliness unaccustomed in the tarahumaras, the floor was sprinkled with water and swept, and each thing in its place: the table, the kitchen utensils, the firewood. Daily, in the afternoons, after leaving work, he bathed in the river from top to toe even if the water was half frozen; *"people say I'm crazy"*; I tried to justify them: *"that is because they take a bath every month"*; *"every year,"* he said laughing in amusement.

It intrigued me that at his age he lived alone; he said he had two girlfriends and showed me a photo in which he appeared in between two girls of slim figure and city look, *"they went to work in the 'citi' and there they got married."* Of his three children he knew nothing since a couple of years ago, when he separated from his wife. Then they offered him a *"gig"* and he came to the south of the sierra to work in the teams that carry out the maintenance of roads; on the way he bought a pair of binoculars, and he was in the habit of climbing the nearby hills to look far away, *"I like to descry my land, from here you can see a large radio antenna that is next to my village."* One day he dropped the binoculars, which hit a rock; one of the lenses smashed to pieces and the focus was damaged, *"however much I move it everything looks 'cloudi'."* He yearned for returning to see his family, but he was like imprisoned in his house, *"if I leave it alone they rob my shop."*

A roaring *"rumble"* of motors interrupted our talk. To a signal of Rosendo we went out secretly, quickly closing the door, *"so that light is not seen."* Three pick up trucks in convoy slipped furtively through the forest; *"they must be drug traffickers,"* he said lowering his voice, *"they must have gone astray, when they don't know they deviate from the way."* There might be the possibility they were Mennonites, as sometimes they go to take them blankets and foods *"to help their tarahumara brethren,"* but, as a rule, they arrived by day. We had to keep ourselves in the darkness, *"if they see us, then they come to ask and get us into trouble."* A good while they were lighting around them with the headlights of the vehicles in high beam, as trying to orient themselves; finally they went back through a narrow dirt road. *"Daily they pass at night,"* the rarámuri assured me. All in the region know that they transport drug shipments toward clandestine landing strips, further north, where the airplanes are waiting; *"they say that they take it to the gringos."* Resigned, he made a mock of the check points the police sets on the roads: *"they already know they're going to find nothing, it's just to simulate."*

Several neighbors have had altercations with the *"chutameros."* Those who he has seen are mestizos, *"they appear to be from here, from the sierra; they go well armed and being nervous, they cannot drink a coffee peacefully."* Some of them are very violent and abusive, compelling the aborigines to guide them through the intricate dirt roads; occasionally they have caused them grave problems. Thrilled, he told me an incident that happened to him months ago: a helicopter of the counter narcotics police flew over his property and he had the unfortunate idea of going out into the yard to observe it with his *"one-eyed"* binoculars; forthwith the crew detected him and also began to scrutinize him with a telescope; they were watching each other for a long time. When he became aware, the aircraft was landing right beside his house stirring up a huge cloud of dust; terrified, he was at the point of running to hide in the forest, but he managed to reason that they would find him easily and it would be *"wurs,"* *"some of them are very bad"*; he barely succeeded in concealing the binoculars under the bed. He was lucky; the policemen were satisfied with inspecting the place, becoming convinced of his innocence on checking the battered lenses. He's never taken them out again, *"it was tough, the fright."*

Some loud knocks on the door woke us up in the middle of the early morning. Outside an unintelligible *"babble"* was heard. It was a handful of drunken tarahumaras; they came from the *"fiesta"* to buy, *"they say they got hungry."* They took sodas, cans of food, crackers and a pack of *"faritos."* As he got into his bed again, Rosendo said to me satisfied: *"at least this lack of sleep was worth it, I earned more than one hundred pesos; anyway I told them the cigarettes are already finished, so they don't come back to disturb."* Till very late the drum that animated the tesgüinada was heard in the distance. Only from time to time could I catch my sleep; under the planks of the floor, mice spent all night making noise.

Like attacked by epilepsy, the feeble little airplane shuddered violently, shaken by the strong air currents. At times it elevated the nose abruptly, ascending toward the sky almost in a vertical line and, then, it descended unexpectedly a long stretch, sinking us into the void as if we were nose-diving; other times it inclined forcefully to the sides, demanding a great effort from the pilot to straighten it back. It was a good while since we had left behind the plateaus, going deeply into the immensity of the canyons; we seemed insects flying in the middle of enormous walls of rock which made the abysses narrow, resembling colossal hands that, arising from the depths, tried to crush us with a fatal applause. When the airplane tilted, we managed to see a thin river running through the bottom of the chasm; the view was at the same time fascinating and terrifying. Before taking off, I asked the pilot if there was any danger of having an accident; he replied with insouciance: *"it's been a long time since anyone has fallen, I don't think it's our turn."* It was a four seat aircraft and we were six persons to travel, *"no problem,"* tranquilized me the audacious steersman, *"we carry few suitcases."* A man wearing a hat was curled up behind my back, in the luggage compartment; he was half drunk and slept giving out sounding snores. An hour later we landed on a little *"runway,"* rather a clearing in the wood, so badly tamped that on touching down we jumped to the top. It took me longer to get out of the plane than it soared again toward its next stop, leaving me all alone in the silent grove. Now I had to walk, the village was not less than six kilometers from the *"airport."*

The courage and ability of the pilots of the sierra to maneuver and meet critical situations, under very precarious flight conditions, is admirable. Many places of the Tarahumara are so inaccessible that the only practical way of reaching them is by air; in some zones there is a regular service of air taxis. Unfortunately, in the southern region, which is the most propitious for drug trafficking, clandestine airstrips have multiplied, hence air patrols of the police and the army are frequent; to thwart them, drug traffickers hang steel cables in strategic places, in an attempt to bring down the surveillance helicopters and airplanes, which has occasioned serious accidents of civilian light aircraft, increasing the unsafety of these flights.

In one of the last aviation mishaps, which shook the whole region, a much esteemed priest perished in the sierra. According to the official report, the pilot suffered a heart attack, causing the plane to fall without control in the middle of the forest, catching fire. Miraculously there was a survivor, the Father's assistant traveling in the back seat, who incomprehensibly, on crashing the airplane against the tops of the pine trees, was thrown into the air through a window and she plunged bumping among the trees, which cushioned her fall. She vaguely remembers that the pilot, suddenly, fell flat on his face upon the controls, and the priest, who was sitting by his side, tried to reanimate him; apparently, when he realized that he was dead, he turned to see her with a grave glance; then she was thrown from the aircraft and blacked out. She never saw them again; severely injured, she was hospitalized the day they buried the charred bodies.

"*Repabé, pabé, pabé; upwards, upwards,*" Tiburcio vehemently encouraged the yoke of oxen that advanced sluggishly, ascending at a slack pace the steep slope, to dig a new furrow from the edge of the parcel; making a great effort he tried to direct the blade of the plow so that the line would be the straightest possible, following the curve of the hillside. He sweated bullets. In spite of his physical strength the task was more and more difficult as the gradient of the hillside augmented gradually and with greater frequency he bumped into huge stones that had to be removed by pushing; besides, a mestizo had lent him the animals and they didn't understand the orders he gave them in tarahumara; he struggled much to control them. The same happened to the mestizos when they borrowed animals from the rarámuris; though few aborigines have economic possibilities to possess draught beasts that facilitate farm work.

After tilling a good part of the plot, the tarahumara stopped for a moment to rest and drink water, waiting to be caught up by his eldest son, aged twelve, and two neighbors who helped him to sow, following him to a short distance with some primitive coas or wooden sticks they used to dig holes in the middle of the furrows, where they deposited several grains of corn, covering them afterwards with earth that they tamped with the foot. The youngest of his four sons, a little child who just recently walked, frolicked with a dog next to a rustic granary, on the limits of his field. With a weary face, Tiburcio contemplated them for an instant with his only eye, while he wiped his forehead; he became one-eyed some years ago, when he was working in a nearby sawmill. After receiving a strong blow with a plank, his eye became infected, "*something dropped inside*"; he could not go to the doctor and the illness got worse. On a bad day it burst suddenly, flowing forth a gush of "*little water*" through the pupil; by all appearances the cornea ulcerated. It was necessary to send him to have the empty sac of his eye removed, which resembled a crushed plum. He never again saw the dawn break on his right side.

Tiburcio's property was situated at the bottom of a narrow valley flanked by two abrupt sierras. He had had to clear the slanting hillsides to establish his crops; yet, as soon as he cut down the original vegetation erosion began; the earth would soon become infertile and then he would have to clear new zones of the forest. Nevertheless, he was lucky; the parcels of other members of his community were located at the edge of a gigantic ravine, and some had such a steep slope that mortal accidents had occurred to fellow peasants who on working them, tripped and went tumbling downhill, plunging into the void.

Feeding is one of the most serious problems the tarahumaras face. To the scarcity of water and the stony nature of the land where they have been relegated, it adds the poor quality of the soil. Even using as fertilizer the dung of the little livestock they possess, the productivity of the fields is low and yield insufficient crops. Although the aborigine has a meager diet throughout the year, and dries a part of his crops to preserve them, the provisions are not enough to satisfy the family requirements until the next agricultural cycle. In winter his situation becomes critical and his chronic hunger reaches desperate levels. The tarahumara is forced to emigrate temporarily in quest of other means of subsistence, getting a job as farm worker in the vegetable plantations of the fertile valleys of Sinaloa, doing piecework for the mestizos, or begging for money on the streets of the cities, bearing abuses and arbitrary actions.

In ancient times, hunting provided an important part of the provisions, but nowadays the majority of the species have become extinct; the small mammals and rodents of a good size are scarce, and seeing a deer hidden amidst the bushes is exceptional. The domestic cattle introduced by the missionaries provided a more reliable source of sustenance, and their products, like milk with which they learned to prepare cheese, diversified his diet. Nevertheless, meat is only consumed in some ceremonies and festivities in which they sacrifice goats or cows to use them as offerings. Wild fruit gathering provides little food, and women and children do it during shepherding. In the wooded zones people gather mushrooms they learn to differentiate from childhood, even if, occasionally, serious intoxications have occurred, and even deaths, on confusing the edible species with poisonous mushrooms. In places where they have easy access to rivers, fishing provides at times a portion of food, and to catch fish they still use ancestral techniques as the construction of small dams; the usage of spears, today with metal tip; and the use of vegetable poisons to paralyze fish, which end up floating *"paunch upwards,"* although this method is not very favored because it affects the young and can finish the shoals.

Notwithstanding the foregoing, agriculture has been the primordial economic activity of the Indian; and, although he sows beans and squash and, in some areas of the canyons where climate is propitious, they grow various fruits and a species of wild coffee, corn is still the main crop and the basis of the nutrition of the tarahumara. For its consumption, it is prepared in many ways; from the tortilla to the esquiate, passing by the pinole, a food well linked to the tarahumaras, which is simply toasted corn ground to a powder. A part of the produce of this cereal is used to elaborate tesgüino, alcoholic beverage considered as sacred since, according to tradition, it is a gift that God gave to the rarámuris. A product of the fermentation of corn, the tesgüino provides a strong nutritional contribution and at the same time causes an initial state of euphoria followed by inebriety. On one occasion I heard a foreigner, who for the first time saw a tesgüino pot, exclaim with displeasure: *it looks like vomit!* Without being pejorative, both for its aspect and its odor, it would be difficult to find a better description; after all, fermentation and digestion are processes with certain similarities.

Given its importance, this beverage has been considered as the cement that sticks the social structure of the rarámuris together. The tesgüino is present in all the gatherings of familiar, social and ceremonial type like the curative and funerary rituals. It is common practice that, in order to facilitate agricultural labor, the families request the help of their neighbors, paying their work with food and tesgüino. These gatherings, called tesgüinadas because they invariably end with the ingestion of that beverage, are the principal mechanism by which individuals associate among themselves, out of the family environment. Besides being a way of recreation, future activities are planned and people interchange information about themes of interest for the whole group. Normally, they not only invite their immediate neighbors, also the residents of the nearby villages participate, which brings about the interaction of people who live in very distant places, and favors the social cohesion of the dispersed indigenous communities. This communal involvement in the diverse engagements of each family, encourages the tesgüinadas taking place on a regular basis and sometimes they carry out two or three per week; in major celebrations, these get-togethers even last two or more days. Since their arrival, the first missionaries reported this type of festivities, and since then, these gave rise to the opinion that the Indians were lazy and irresponsible, and spent all their time getting drunk. These judgments, precipitate and extremist, feed on ancestral racial prejudices, and are born out of the ignorance of the fundamental role that these reunions play in the life of the rarámuris.

Nevertheless, it would be dishonest to cover up the problems that the tesgüinadas arouse. Under the influence of alcohol, aggressions of sexual type, like rapes, are often committed; other times inebriety prevents the ceremony or the programmed work from being carried out; quarrels and fights are also frequent, which at its worst, end up in homicides because, owing to the isolation of the villages, it is not difficult that an injury inflicted in such circumstances turns out to be mortal. Thus happened to a tarahumara young man seriously wounded in a tesgüinada of a remote hamlet. With a leg almost cut off by a slash with a machete and a deep cut in the abdomen, with difficulty he was carried to a railroad station. Although he could board the second class train, he didn't make the hospital; he bled to death on the way. His relatives got the corpse off at the next stop to return to bury him in his land. Only a puddle of blood remained on the floor of the car; while the janitor cleaned it making an expression of repugnance, he muttered, exasperated: *"lousy Indians, they only came to leave their filth here."*

In one of the most dramatic cases, attended in a rural clinic, a woman who carried her little son on her back, completely drunk, fell backwards onto a bonfire and fell asleep; the child suffered extensive burns and carbonizations that caused his death. Even though inebriety is to be considered as a spiritual journey which takes one to intangible celestial worlds or to an intimate contact with the gods, it would be grotesque to pretend it justifies atrocities such as the preceding

one. Even from an indigenous perspective, this conduct is reprehensible, as is demonstrated by the insistent exhortations of the governors in order that their communities refrain from committing such excesses.

The negative effects of alcoholism are indisputable and favoring its diffusion is absurd, knowing beforehand the harm it causes the body and mind of the individual, and the grave social conflicts it generates, which, in extreme cases, lead to chaos. Nevertheless, one cannot *"satanize"* the tarahumaras; although many of them fall into alcoholism, this problem is not exclusive of the indigenous groups; it is present in all the history of humankind, including the modern civilization which, besides, suffers from a fondness for taking narcotics and psychotropic drugs. On the other hand, the acts of savagery committed under the influence of these substances are more frequent in the cities, where they have reached unsuspected degrees of cruelty and brutality. Of course, this is neither a consolation nor an apology, but it puts things in their place. Insofar as they manage to control or eradicate these evils from a society, a real progress enabling the intellectual and spiritual amelioration of the human being will be achieved.

Another argument, on which the scorn toward the indigenous culture is upheld, is the alleged squandering of resources for ceremonial purposes, which lacerates the family economics, hindering saving to improve their standard of living. The indigenous system of production is based on community labor because it offers an additional work force, non commercial, which compensates for the lack of more sophisticated production means; but its greatest importance lies in establishing ways of living together which facilitate the integration of the individual into his community. This practice is complemented with the ceremonial rituals that, besides connecting him with his mythic and celestial world, build a hierarchic order which gives moral support to his society and grants recognition to its more capable members, promoting a solid cultural identity. The rules of urbanities oblige the most prosperous families to help the poorest ones, sharing their food and resources, to favor the economic equilibrium and the social equality. But the rarámuri is not only committed to his fellow men; his existence is, unavoidably, linked to the Universe.

An ancient tarahumara legend holds that they are the pillars of the world by divine command, and their behavior affects the well-being of the earth and its people. Although the content of the story is metaphoric, its precepts have profound implications in the daily life and force the awakening of the social conscience, delegating an enormous responsibility to its members on making them realize that the individual acts influence inevitably the community. According to this crucial religious belief, the Indian must help to preserve the earth and take only what is necessary to subsist and protect himself; besides, the relationship with his divinities requires of reciprocity and, in gratitude, he must return in offerings a little of the benefits received. A person who abuses, accumulating riches and forgetting to share, will provoke the divine wrath, suffering as punishment evils and diseases. The ceremonial expense is a tribute to life.

The indigenous governors constantly emphasize in their sermons this inescapable obligation they have as a people. The tarahumara strives to help his fellowmen, emulating his deities; like the sun which bravely rises everyday in the sky to lavish the light and the heat that make the crops ripen. For the rarámuri, social acceptance and living together with his fellowmen are more valuable than the accumulation of goods; and since he depends on the community to survive and get personal satisfaction, he has the commitment of working and watching over the welfare of the group. Such an idea is shared by many aboriginal societies of the planet which have instituted mechanisms of communal support to balance the social conditions of their members, putting the common good before the individual. This approach is radically opposed to the current tendency of modern civilization to satisfy egoism and vanity, procuring individual benefit even at the expense of damaging the others or the earth itself.

The ceremonial expense of the tarahumara is a minimal loss compared to the obsessive squandering of consumerism, in which life is mortgaged to get comfort and superfluous material wealth that do not manage to satisfy the essential needs of the human soul. The enthusiastic financial reports of the rich countries which boast about an uncertain economic boom are opprobrious, since they consider the commercial issue as the only parameter to evaluate the well-being of a society; omitting the calamities it suffers, like the alarming increase in violence, drug addiction, moral degradation and family disintegration, which lead the human being toward social isolation; condemning him to sink into the sterile solitude and the spiritual void, denying him the possibility of being happy. History demonstrates that opulence gives rise to frivolity and arrogance; before considering ourselves as a superior culture, we could ask ourselves if it is worth sacrificing the spirit in exchange for a handful of luxuries and banalities.

The more furious they appeared, the more they gloated over hurting them by twisting their noses or pulling out their eyes; then their ire waned and they got satisfied with sinking their cheeks or aging them by wrinkling their forehead. They were like shadowgraphs that in their unpredictable fluttering on their faces, disfigured them, swaying to the capricious rhythm of the flames that, in big igneous laps, threatened to escape from the enormous bonfire to set fire to the crowd that dared to congregate around it. Two drums and a violin animated the tesgüinada. Gourds full of liquor passed from hand to hand until empting avidly into the throats that, at times, celebrated noisily roaring with laughter. Some people chatted in a low voice taking refuge in the penumbra; others danced stumbling next to the fire; a few were dumped on the edges, rolled in dust, vanquished by the alcohol. Sat on the comfy mattress that their soft skirts formed, the women fully participated in the get-together; and though they showed greater moderation in their behavior, their enthusiasm and diligence were an indispensable part of the celebration, which gathered almost all the village.

Caught between sanity and dementia, I contemplated ecstatically the magical play of lights and shadows. Leaning against the trunk of a tree, I enjoyed the pleasant adventure of lying down on the ground and feeling the smooth texture of cool earth, which crumbled among the fingers of my hands. Half a liter of tesgüino was beginning to dull my senses and had overflowed my vesical capacity. Urged by physiology, I moved away from the group staggering in the blackness, looking for a place to relieve myself. I wound up at the side of a small semicylindrical dome which operated as a portable classroom of the shelter-school. When I approached the wall, a gentle noise coming from the inside and resembling the scratch of an animal called my attention. With curiosity I looked into the window and, in the light of the moon that entered through the doorway without a door, I managed to see a couple lying on the floor, amongst the desk chairs of the pupils. Both were dressed and, on moving, their clothes rubbed against each other. The woman was lying with the face upward, with her fluffy skirts raised up to her waist, showing her fleshy, separated, thighs glistening on reflecting the silvery light of the night; the countless folds of her dress draped spilling to the sides, shaping a pair of fans of unthinkable symmetry. Mounted in between her legs, with the hat on, the man toiled on the soft hips of the girl, submerging rhythmically into that sea of flounces.

It all happened in a minute. Embarrassed by my involuntary interference, even my urinary reflex was frightened away. I tried to withdraw in silence, but the clumsiness of an awkward movement uncovered me. On noticing my presence the woman got up abruptly and, pulling down her numerous underskirts all at once, she left running toward the bonfire, mingling with the crowd. The man crouched down in a corner and stayed immobile, hidden in the dark. Disconcerted, I walked away whistling unworriedly, pretending nothing had happened. I couldn't help spending the rest of the soirée spying on the attendance out of the corner of my eyes, trying to catch unawares some revealing gesture; it was in vain, there were only glassy stares with an expression of absence, taciturn figures with melancholic grimaces, and swollen faces that let out resounding guffaws, surrendering themselves to euphoria.

The tesgüinadas are the socially accepted realm in which the majority of the couples begin their sexual life. Many of the current matrimonies started their relationship at these events; even the mestizos who cohabit with indigenous women, *"abducted"* their concubine when they were invited to one of these reunions. Between the tarahumara couples there is no formal courtship in the occidental way, and romanticism, as it is conceived in modern civilization, is practically absent. After their carnal union the couple live together *"on trial"* for a year; if their characters are compatible, they continue the relationship, if not, they simply separate and look for another mate. Virginity is little valued by the Indian; a woman who already has a child won't have the least problem finding a man who agrees to live with her. Nevertheless, it is very likely that a woman with several children is rejected, not because of moral questions, but because of the economic burden the maintenance of her children represents.

The belief that the tarahumaran celebrations are real orgies where there is great promiscuity, and adultery, incest and rapes are seen with indifference, has been disseminated since the colonial epoch. Reality is not that simplistic and catastrophic; it is undeniable that, under the influence of inebriety, in these get-togethers, excesses of sexual nature are committed, which, far from passing unnoticed, provoke serious interpersonal disagreements and originate rancor and disputes, ending in violent incidents when the offenses of previous tesgüinadas are claimed. However, just like any human society, the rarámuris appreciate the family a lot as a fundamental part of the social structure and they strive to give it stability and health, for the survival of the group depends on that. In its bosom, children are formed, teaching them values that allow them to enjoy life and find a sense to the human presence in the Universe, showing them a way toward happiness.

The governors exhort their communities insistently to respect themselves and avoid conflictive situations that disturb the social coexistence. The discretion and prudence of the tarahumaras for not meddling in the life of others are well known; but when conditions that they perceive as risky for the conjugal harmony of the couples of a hamlet emerge, for instance: the widowhood of one of its members or the arrival of new members to the community, above all if it has to do with women of marriageable age, it is common that the neighbors try to persuade them to find a partner who offers them an emotional balance as soon as possible, and avoid becoming a potential factor of instability for the other couples. In spite of that, polygamy is not obligatorily censurable, and some cases occur without the slightest problem.

The communal order of the rarámuris takes us back to the most primitive stages of social organization; to the dawn of human time when natural laws conditioned the behavior of the individual, focusing it to satisfy basic and real necessities. Every member executes activities biologically determined. The man, given his greater physical strength, performs the heaviest work like building abodes, the agricultural labors or the transportation of provisions. The woman takes care of housework, elaborating articles that demand patience and dexterity, and she is the fundamental pillar on which rests the family structure; this role is widely recognized and respected, even without being a matriarchy. The indigenous women value their social position devoting their best effort to it, considering it an important part of a joint responsibility to move the group ahead. They neither suffer from absurd feelings of inferiority nor do they wear themselves out claiming fictitious liberties; in an attitude completely opposite to the current feminist tendency, they delight in their differences with men, instead of insisting in obtaining a nonexistent equality. In a world conference of indigenous women, where members of the most diverse ethnic groups of the entire globe participated, a similar stance was openly stated and they declared, proudly, to be the bastions of their cultural heritage, for it is them who fight the most to preserve their traditions, refusing to abandon their typical attire and their various languages. I recall a significant talk with an elderly woman, who worked clapping balls of dough to make tortillas, rounding them with the utmost care before cooking them on a blackened griddle. When I asked her why her husband did not make tortillas, she answered smiling in a tone of elemental logic: *"that is just fo' a woman; men are good fo' other things."*

Nothing in the Universe indicates equality must exist among the beings inhabiting it; on the contrary, the great constant of Cosmos is the infinite diversity, which overwhelms and fascinates the mind. Reality is conclusive; from the genetic to the psychological level, passing by the physical, the physiological and the social, the differences between both sexes are abysmal, and they condition the function that belongs to each one to fulfill. Not acknowledging such an irrefutable fact is a stubbornness born out of ignorance and the stupid concept that being different is equivalent to being inferior, on which is also based the racism, which has been so detrimental to the indigenous people. Fewer times has prejudice been so devastating for a society. If we stopped squandering time absorbed in futile arguments, trying to define what nature has already defined, and we devoted ourselves to exalt our differences, learning to live together and respect each other, fostering transcendental values like authenticity, honesty, altruism and sincere commitment, the prospects for the future of the human being would be more promising.

From the edge of the abyss it seemed a minute toy house abandoned at the foot of the imposing wall of rock, lost in the immensity of the range of mountains which extended to the horizon like sharpened backbones of dinosaurs that, having plunged into the chasm, were lying prone incrusted in the earth, sleeping an interminable sleep. A little flock of sheep grazed around the cabin, adorning it with minuscule woolen pompoms, black and white. It took me more than an hour to descend the impressive slope, stumbling along when slipping on the elusive little stones that carpeted the slanting trail. The afternoon was dying and the light of the sun had escaped from the bottom of the canyons. It was the end of long day's journey traveling over indigenous communities, giving out medicament and promoting the cultivation of vegetables to improve the family diet. That morning, in a clearing of the grove, between two villages, I had had a revealing encounter with a young Jesuit priest; wearing blue jeans, checked cowboy shirt, huaraches and a straw hat, the only thing that identified him as a religious was a large wooden crucifix that was hanging from his neck; he was making a pastoral visit on foot carrying on his shoulder a satchel woven out of multicolored worsted yarn where he took the bare essentials for celebrating, rustically, the mass. The unexpected coincidence enabled me to enter briefly in the intimacy of his world; he was seeking to save the souls, I was after the bodies. When I continued on my way, crossing alone through the forest, I could not stop wondering if it was valid to tear apart the human being like this.

It had almost gotten dark when I arrived at the house. Gumersindo, the owner, had just returned from the village and with great effort unloaded several packages tied to the backs of two burros which patiently bore the shaking. He had gone to stock up with supplies and to deal with a matter of someone who *"had been harassing him very much."* A mestizo of the hamlet wanted to divest him of his parcel; as *"he had connections"* with some municipal officials, he intended to take it away from him by perversely manipulating the law. *"Says we don't have papers; what does one know about it?"*; countless generations of his family had lived in the place without having to worry about deeds or lot limits. To defend himself he sought the help of superior authorities, and he spent his time taking them cheese, pinole and other simple presents to win their goodwill; now, every time he came across the mestizo, this one disguisedly insulted him saying loudly as he passed by: *"damn Indians, they are very sly, and they have such a gift of gab, the bastards."* I prepared to leave when the tarahumara invited me insistently to stay there that night, *"it might sting you an animal in the thicket"*; Jovita, his wife, had arranged with great care several blankets on a coarse rustic wooden bed dumped in a narrow room that served as warehouse; even though one managed to see the faint light of the stars through the crevices of the roof, absolute darkness reigned inside. I entered with distrust, hoping there wouldn't be some scorpion or a snake hidden amongst so many sacks and boxes piled up against the walls; much to my regret, as I crossed the doorway I felt a shudder, and I remembered the words of the ancient missionaries, it was like entering a sepulture.

"Take a photo of my old man so that you give it to me as a keepsake," Jovita asked me the following day, while we had pea soup and tortillas for breakfast, *"he is already old and it won't take long before he dies"*; Gumersindo said nothing, he ate placidly with a kind smile on the lips, which gave his aged face an expression of nobleness and wisdom. He didn't know how old he was, *"cause then who would take you to be registered,"* they could be more than sixty; his wife looked pretty young, maybe some thirty. They had procreated a little girl, aged ten, and a son, aged seven, who had just began to help his father with farm work. In time, I discovered that such a disparity between the ages of the couples was not something rare. Equally surprising was to find numerous marriages of indigenous women with mestizo men, contradicting the popular saying that tarahumara women don't get involved with mestizos because they fear catching diseases. On one occasion I asked a young rarámuri woman half *"mestizoed,"* who worked serving in a communal store, if she wouldn't have any objection in marrying an old man; mischievously she answered: *"I go with ya doesn't matter ya're fifty, just that ya're not married."*

In the luminous clarity of the morning we were descending toward the bottom of an isolated and inhospitable ravine, whose hillsides were so steep and arid that it was hard to conceive how someone could live in it. Gumersindo had requested that I go to see a relative: *"she is much deteriorated; she lives here just behind the hill."* It took us more than an hour to get to a modest house made of adobe and stone. Alarmed by the presence of a stranger, four women waited in front of the door: an old woman, a medium aged lady, a young woman and a girl who laughed grotesquely while a trickle of saliva drained from her mouth moistening her blouse; she had the absent stare of the mentally retarded people. The patient was lying on a bed, in one of the rooms; she was a young lady of some twenty five years of age, and was very drawn and had her skin *"pale as a candle."* She complained of fatigue, dizziness and a lack of strength; her problem appeared to be limited to severe malnutrition and anemia. She had several months feeding badly, besides the physical debilitation caused by trying to cultivate a rachitic field of maize in the sterile ravine and shepherding a handful of skinny goats. For some unknown reason, after finishing school, the two young women, who were cousins, went to take refuge with their relatives in this isolated corner. *"That they don't wanna know anything about men because they are very wicked; that they beat women,"* Gumersindo said, confused, *"if they haven't even had a boyfriend."* It seemed so ridiculous to have to imagine this remote place as the last bastion of unflinching feminism. When we returned Jovita told me worried: *"that's all that schools are good fo', who knows what things do they put into their head,"* and she added, disheartened: *"they don't listen to me, I tell them to find a good partner who looks after them well, that they have their family; or else they're going to end up alone."*

What did you dream? It was the first thing José asked me on waking up, sitting down in front of me with an inquisitive look; still stunned by somnolence I only managed to answer: *"nothing, I already forgot it,"* and I remained a good while in silence trying to clear up my thoughts, lain on the floor on a petate he had lent me as a mattress. Disappointed by the succinct reply, the rarámuri started to roll up the other *"beds"* of the family, arranging them at the back of the room. His wife was making tortillas on a griddle from which emanated a white column of smoke that flooded the place creating an atmosphere of irreality. The delicate light of dawn arrived in an imperceptible way, slowly infiltrating into the darkest corners, filling the enclosure with a beautiful luminosity and uncovering several clusters of objects hung from the ceiling which, in the blackness of the night, were mistaken for specters that were lying in ambush at the heights, disrupting rest. Hens clucked pursuing themselves through the yard, and in the distance the soft trill of birds was heard. Reanimated by the cool quietude of the morning, I contemplated, enraptured, the first rays of the sun which penetrated insolently through the holes of the roof and the walls, drawing small golden circles in the inside of the room. The ambiance was charged with new and heady aromas that ignited secret sensations, long ignored. It seemed to me as having woken up into a dream, or been dreaming, still.

And they always asked me the same when I stayed to sleep with tarahumaras. Then I knew that, often, they visited themselves at daybreak to talk about what they had dreamed. At first I didn't comprehend this unusual interest in dreams, until I learned of the important meaning they attribute to them. It all turns around the soul; but not that one of the Christian religion, but a purely indigenous concept, pre-Columbian, forged in Nature, and whose root disappears into the dawn of human knowledge. With this idea the tarahumara tries to explain to himself the physical, mental and emotional phenomena that affect the individual, and it is fundamental to give a sense to his existence and understand his relationship with the environment that surrounds him, because it is associated with the essential worries of life. Although the origin of this concept is, undoubtedly, autochthonous, given the influence that is patent in other areas and some linguistic parallelisms, it is possible to conjecture with foundation that the Christian notion of the soul helped the rarámuri to clearly define his own conception, and even enriched it with new elements like the Devil, personage that was unknown to him and which served to interpret the unexpected arrival of the white man, whom, for his evilness, haughtiness and extreme voracity, he considered a spawn of the very Lucifer himself.

The field anthropologic studies have been able to elucidate with certain precision the cosmovision that rules the indigenous mentality, but at the same time they have determined the existence of a great heterogeneity in the ideas, owing both to the fact that there is not an institutional system of education, therefore the concepts are transmitted informally in the bosom of the family permitting individual variation; and the isolation of the scattered communities, which favors the appearance of discrepancies. The tarahumaran conception could be summarized in a simple outline: the body is merely a temporary shelter where souls dwell and protect themselves during their stay on the earth. Identified with breath and respiration, living depends on them because they provide heat, strength and movement to the body and take care of it. They are classified in large and small, and, according to their hierarchy, they reside in the chest, the head or the joints. There is no general consensus regarding their number, but many believe that the man possesses three large souls and the woman four, because she needs greater vigor to exert the faculties belonging to her sex, like procreating children. The large souls grow and mature with the person, becoming strong and reliable, whereas the small ones and those of the children are frail and irresponsible. All living beings, plants and animals, have a soul, and even the wind, which is considered an invisible being roaming over the globe.

In accordance with the rarámuri beliefs, the diverse corporal states like inebriety, sleep, illness and death are conditioned by the acts of the souls and their correlation with the body. When someone imbibes tesgüino, its smell displeases his large souls and makes them go away from the body leaving it in the charge of the small ones, hence a drunk behaves like a child, unable to walk or speak correctly, and he is left exposed to the influence of the devil, who advises him to misbehave. On digesting and eliminating the tesgüino the souls return and soberness comes back. Sleep also occurs when the souls leave the body, and it is preceded by the prolonged exhalations of yawns, which announce the departure. Dreams come about when they encounter other souls, and they are considered real happenings lived by these during their extracorporeal tours. For the Indian, the universe in which souls evolve on leaving the body is diametrically opposite to the one we perceive when we are awake, as if we had inverse perspectives of the same reality. Thus, for them the sun would be the moon; spring, autumn; and the unfathomable abysses, craggy sierras. It's easy to comprehend such a deduction, derived from the analysis of the dreams whose events appear to take place by day although, regularly, they occur while we sleep by night. Anybody has had this kind of experiences.

Who has not lived that singular moment between subconsciousness and wakefulness, when we don't even dare move so as not to break the spell, so as to prolong our stay in that hidden corner of existence, full of confused and unknown emotions that make us quiver intensely, and

which on opening our eyes inexorably escape towards oblivion, making vain efforts to retain them in our memory? What a lot of unsuspected feelings seize the spirit on returning from a journey through the intriguing world of dreams. What soul has not suffered an outburst of anguish and sorrow after its fleeting stay in unknown and gloomy places where it wanders desolate; or after the terrifying encounter with supernatural or diabolic beings? Who has not felt the disquietude and the nostalgia of a bitter return to the past; or the sweet happiness of the fulfilled desire, which, on our waking up, vanishes?

In view of the incredible variety of situations and so vivid perceptions that occur in this ethereal environment, there is logic in the conclusion of the frank, ingenious and receptive mind of the Indian, whose fecund imagination leads him to conceive the existence of a spiritual kingdom inhabited by a multitude of fantastic beings, good and evil, who interact with the souls, affecting their vitality. These influences would explain one of his most worrisome questions: illness. When souls leave during the dreams they are exposed to serious dangers because they could be captured by the Devil or his henchmen, like the coyotes and the sorcerers, which prowl around constantly in search of victims. A person gets sick when his soul is abducted by some of these personages. The most serious and urgent cases are caused by the sorcerers, who usually cook and eat them within a few days, provoking the death of the sick person; on other occasions, they introduce objects in the body to alter its function and cause diseases; they can, for instance, tie invisible wires to the hips of pregnant women to hinder the parturition.

Other beings, vaguely defined, are *"the people of the water"* who dwell under the aquatic currents, which could be harmful if they come to catch the souls of whoever gets frightened near their dominions. It is very likely that this belief has been introduced by the colonists since it has an extraordinary similarity to an old custom deeply rooted in the ancient villages of the country, which warns that when a child falls asleep or someone scares by the banks of a river or stream, his companions, on leaving, must go repeating the name of the person and calling him out loud: *"come do not stay,"* to prevent his soul from remaining imprisoned in the water and getting sick; if this happens it will be necessary *"to cure it of fright"* to make it come back.

There is another prominent group of beings, personified by plants, which can protect or damage the souls of the individual depending on his behavior towards them. By the magic powers and the curative virtues that are conferred to it, the most important is the jícuri or peyote, which demands an exhausting ritual to grant its favors and provide protection. It is regarded as sacred, considering it brother of the great Sun God, and its effects are interpreted as divine communication. And with good reason; just the same as other hallucinogenic substances, like the lysergic acid and some mushrooms, its alkaloids act overflowing the mind and senses, distorting the perception of time and space, fusing them into a unique single dimension in which all barriers disappear. Yesterday and now, life and death, get lost in the unfathomable sensation of being everlastingly united to eternity and the absolute. Depending on the temperament of the person, the experience will take him to the chaos of madness or the sublimation of mysticism. It is interesting to notice that amongst its effects is the one of annulling libido; therefore the aborigines consider that sexual abstinence is an indispensable requisite to be able to worship it.

In modern civilization an excessive, and even morbid, attention has been given to the worship of peyote, surely for its own tendency to become fond of psychotropic drugs. It is significant that the main interest of many anthropologists and some physicians who frequent the indigenous communities is in having access to these rituals in order to experiment with *"transcendental experiences which reveal an esoteric universal wisdom."* Such was the case with a French ethnologist, who, after ingesting an overdose of peyote during a huichol pilgrimage, suffered a serious attack of dementia, undressing himself and running crazily amidst the bushes; to avoid injury it was necessary to tie him up until the crisis eased off.

Nowadays this practice, which survived the repression of the Holy Inquisition by taking refuge in clandestinity, is on a clear decline in the Tarahumara and it is extremely difficult to find where to witness it. One of the reasons could be the difficulty in getting the plant, native to the arid zones in the center and north of the country; but it is more feasible that due to the iron discipline that such a rigorous tradition demands, the new generations, exposed to powerful external influences, are abandoning it. A tarahumara old man, well versed in these questions, explained that the ability to communicate and invoke the spirit of the peyote is a gift you are born with, and could easily be lost because of bad behavior and envies. A young religious, with several years of professing in an order assigned to the Tarahumara, described plainly her own experience when she was invited, unexpectedly, to participate in a *"fiesta."* To her surprise, the reunion was carried out surreptitiously in a hidden ravine, in the denseness of the forest. Until the leader of the ceremony started to rub forcefully a notched stick she realized he was a *"rasper"* and recognized the kind of ritual he was performing; she couldn't avoid receiving one of the little bits of peyote they were handing out to all the attendants, and had no choice but eating it. Nevertheless, due to the scarcity of the product and *"the fear they have of it,"* the portions were very small. Smiling, mischievous, the nun said disappointed: *"you don't even feel a thing."*

The veneration of the peyote was very spread out in the desert regions of northern México and southern United States from where it is native. Not many decades ago it was used by the mestizo families of scant resources to prepare curative potions; the grandparents still recall their extravagant metaphysical adventures, and they relate that quite a few *"remained up there."* It was known by the Aztecs, whose language derives its Spanish name; but, doubtlessly, the rite reached its maximum development with the huichol, who still undertake an arduous annual pilgrimage to obtain it and carry out elaborate ceremonies. It is very likely the tarahumaras have acquired it from them, as it is suggested by the fact that they name it with almost identical words, in addition

to certain notable coincidences in the rituals and their objective. Perhaps the tepehuanos, who had extensive relations with both ethnic groups, took part in the transmission of such knowledge.

In the indigenous catalogue of diseases there is another category of illnesses that only affect the body and are more benign, although if they get worse or prolonged they become deadly because they annoy the souls, which could decide to abandon it. The contact with the souls of the dead or with food touched by them produces digestive disorders. Sexual relations with mestizos would also bring about bodily afflictions. In children death by dehydration is frequent, caused by vomits and diarrheas that *"dry them up on the inside,"* which are attributed to the *"falling in of the soft spot,"* a concept taken from the mestizos, whose remedies are considered more effective to treat it.

The complicated cosmovision of the rarámuri originates a series of rituals and ceremonies that have great significance in his life because they are destined to prevent and cure diseases. In them it is patent a strong presence of foreign elements that, unquestionably, were contributed by the missionaries. One of the things that impressed the Jesuits the most, when they had just arrived at the Tarahumara, was observing the use of crosses during the celebrations, with a very different meaning from the Christian though: representing man, the dead, God and even, in time, the Devil. Apparently, the new religious teachings motivated the Indians to ascribe them additional properties of preventive and curative type. Still at present, sorcerers use crucifixes in their rites, and include symbols and movements that reproduce this shape. It wouldn't be venturous to attribute this interpretation to defective translations of liturgical phrases such as: *"heal the soul,"* which fit perfectly within their conception of illness.

The preventive practices go from the simple placement of chilies, thorny branches or icons of saints around the houses, or carrying medals and crucifixes; to the adoption of peyote plants, to invoke its protection, or the performance of little ceremonies with offerings to avoid the rage of the Devil and other malevolent beings. Rituals are also made to protect the crops and livestock, in which sermons are delivered to encourage them to be productive and accept their destiny of serving as food to man. When in spite of all the preventive measures a person falls ill, and one suspects the intervention of evil beings, the services of a sorcerer are required; this one, among other characteristics, must have the quality of *"dreaming well,"* for it is in dreams that he locates the place where the soul of the sick person is trapped; besides he must know how to take out the objects that other sorcerers introduce inside the body, and become acquainted with the elemental healing ritual which includes the administration of agave and tesgüino potions, the use of crucifixes, massages and suctions, the transfer of souls with the breath to fortify the body, and deliver brief speeches to revitalize and gladden the souls of the sick person.

The individual dies right in the very moment when all the souls of his body leave forever; this one transforms again into clay, from which God originally created man. The souls of the dead enter, irrevocably, the inverse and metaphysical territory that the living only perceives in dreams; suffering an inexplicable intrinsic change that turns them harmful for the inhabitants of *"this world."* After their death, the souls start a swift tour through the sites where they were in life, to recover their hair, nails and tears that they must present before God. This belief, which many consider autochthonous of the rarámuris, was actually taken from the mestizos, and it is common in villages of various regions of the country. I recall the accounts of a distant relative, very old, born in an ancient hacienda of the isolated deserts of northeastern México, who narrated how people took great care to keep their nails and hair they cut, because on dying they would have to come back to pick them up and retrace their steps, in order to render an account to God. All the time she objected, angrily, how impracticable a trip to the past would be for someone as old as her, with almost a century of experiences, and she concluded grumbling with disdain: *"where was one going to keep so many locks; that was pure insanity; otiose people no longer knew what to make up."*

On finishing their itinerary, which men make in three days and women in four, the souls return to gather the offerings their relatives give them to help them in the other life, and rise to heaven to be judged by God. They believe in the existence of places analogous to Paradise and Hell, where in accordance with their conduct in life the dead go to; but, unlike Christianity which augurs the eternal suffering of sinful souls in the flames of Hell, the wicked are sent to the Devil for him to destroy them. Some sins are punished by embodying in wild animals that roam by night damaging the living. Both Heaven and the subterranean dominions of Satan are conceived as a sort of enclosures with several stories, through which the souls pass; Heaven, in particular, would be supported by huge columns that rest on the confines of the earth, which they imagine as a disc surrounded by water, *"like a tortilla or like a drum."* The good souls would ascend to God to help him for eternity.

Nevertheless, the souls of the dead are very reluctant to break the familial bonds and try to take with them their relatives, appearing to them in dreams to convince them. One of the major dangers is the sadness that seizes people after the death of a relative, for yearning can cause souls to wish to leave the body to go with the deceased. This explains the impassive behavior of the Indian before his dead; to avoid the risk of also dying, he must try to gladden and be indifferent to grief, dancing and joking in the tesgüinadas. For his own good, he must resign himself as soon as possible to his loss, counting on the support of the community. For that several funeral ceremonies, considered obligatory, are carried out, which have as main objectives the satisfaction of the basic needs of the deceased, while they adapt to the other life, and the protection of the living from the dead. Normally a ritual is performed annually, up to three years for men and four for women, and end with a final ceremony more elaborate and costly. At those ceremonies they present offerings of food, clothes and daily use tools, placing them next to wooden crosses that represent the deceased; the offering is made in front of them, sprinkling them with potions of agave, tesgüino and pinole, at the same time a brief sermon is delivered in order to persuade them to accept their new condition and to not to annoy the living. There are, as well, music and dances in which, it is presumed, the dead participate; and they finish with a little procession and a long tesgüinada.

The last ceremony, which settles the obligations of the living with the deceased, includes the same activities of the previous ones and adds exclusive elements which denote a clear influence of the catholic religion, such as drawing ash crosses in the forehead of the attendants, in a ritual that has irrefutable similarities to the celebration of Ash Wednesday; and not only for its physical representation, but for the meaning they confer to it, because even though the tarahumaras are also in the habit of scattering ashes around their houses and food, convinced that they will protect them by scaring away the dead, it is evident that in the indigenous soul echoed the frightful phrase that initiates the Lent abstinence and move us to humility and reflection, on reminding us of the fragility of life: *"dust you are, and to dust you will return."*

Nobody wanted to show me where they interred the dead. When I asked them they evaded me shutting themselves in a suspicious silence, as protecting an inviolable secret. Even the teacher of the shelter-school, a tarahumara young man very mestizoed, refused looking at me distrustfully, puzzled by the unusual request; in his refusal there was a hint of fear. Disheartened, one afternoon I went out to wander alone through the forest, traversing toward the other side of the ravine. As I passed over the stream I found the children of the school taking a bath seminude; they jumped in group plunging into the milky water of a pond formed under a small waterfall, making a tremendous commotion that disturbed the tranquility of the grove. As I walked away, their shouts got gradually quenched, mingled with the sighing of the wind that agitated the crowns of the pines. Unexpectedly the trees began to appear blackened, with all the bark scorched; somebody had burned the place to make a clearing, and it still smelled of burnt resin. Suddenly, astonished, I discovered a loose blouse hanging from a branch; at first I confused it with a person, but when I saw its long sleeves swinging in the air, as wanting to embrace the trunk, I supposed it had been forgotten there. Nevertheless, as I advanced, I found more clothes in vivid colors hanging from the trees like Christmas ornaments, and I had the strange impression of being surrounded by tarahumaras, perched on the branches! A few steps ahead I was stunned as I bumped into the first graves; they were covered with piles of stones, and had a small wooden cross at the head, from which hung rosaries, necklaces and gourds; around them there were palm baskets with offerings, pots, garments and even a tiny drum.

I sat in the middle of the graveyard and my imagination took flight, fascinated by the enigmatic custom of leaving some belongings of the deceased on the tombs so that he could use them in his new existence, serving at the same time as a last link with the living, to preserve the familial bonds in spite of his absence. I delighted in remembering the days of childhood at grandmother's house, when our curiosity overcame fear and we insisted on spending the nights watching the Day of the Dead Altar to see them come and take the offerings; invariably, fatigue made us sleepy and we ended up dreaming about the smell of guavas and cempasúchil, about the skeletons of bread and the skulls of sugar that on the forehead carried our names. When we woke up in the morning, evaporation played a mean joke on us as we noticed that the level of the water in the glasses had diminished. Our grandparents filled our astonishment to the brim as they approached stealthily to assure us, in a low voice, that the thirsty souls of the deceased had drunk it.

These beliefs, so rooted in the aboriginal people and so incomprehensible for our modern materialistic mentality, seemed to me the pillars of the indigenous mysticism. Unable to arrive, physically, to heaven, and not habituated to religious introspection, the rarámuri can only reach God in the full contact with Nature, which instills in the spirit a totalizing notion of the universe, where all that exists lives in a permanent change, integrating an unshakable and eternal whole that leaves no room for total death. So confused and inexplicable concepts can only be discerned giving them a mystical sense, and would have engendered animism and the ideas about reincarnation that some ancestral cultures still preserve. I wondered if the primitive man would have known some forgotten language to communicate with *"the other world"*; some secret knowledge that would mitigate the terrible abandonment that brings about the death of a loved one, and the heartrending agony of not knowing which has been his final destination. Inevitably I arrived to the anguishing and perennial question: Where do the dead go? Is it true that there is a God, and a Heaven to which the good souls soar to be happy in eternity; or are we condemned to putrefy in the bottom of a cold grave which pitilessly devours our dreams and desires, transforming us into nothing? Can the faith in a future reunion deceive hope and soothe the pain of losing those whom you have loved so dearly?

Recalling the sorrow the rarámuris manifested when the sickness of some relative confronted them with fatality, contemplating the offerings which expressed the love that joined them to the absentees, I answered myself disillusioned that there is no possible consolation for the irremediable. The man of yesterday, of today, of all times, has always been helpless before the brutal arrival of death. And yet, it has been this impenetrable mystery what has forged our spirit since the immemorial epoch when the human conscience was born. In the adversity of its terrifying existence our fortitude has tempered and we have learned humility on understanding the insignificance of our ephemeral stay on earth; giving a profound meaning to the brevity of life, which barely give us enough time to fill ourselves with beautiful and good experiences, sole

baggage we shall carry in the soul. It is this overwhelming reality what unmasks the ridiculous futility of our mundane efforts to attain everlasting glory. Only by leaving through our acts a discreet and beautiful trace in other souls, shall we be able to aspire to transcend, for a moment, into the perpetuity of time. In an amazing paradox, Death has also been our misunderstood ally to preserve existence on the planet; for it is an indispensable part of the cycle of life. We need to evolve, truly, taking a new and revolutionary approach to the meaning of our passage on earth; to learn to live for not fearing dying. After all, if even stars die, it is really stupid to pretend that we, vile sacks of bones, be immortal. Nowadays, wrapped in an artificial world, away from the true Universe, almost converted into gods swollen with pride and self-sufficiency; how to comprehend life? How to explain to ourselves Death?

Absorbed in so many existentialist digressions, I didn't notice that the light of evening was fading rendering the forest somber; creating an eerie and mysterious ambiance that was accentuated by the gloomy ululating of the freezing wind. The sun was setting on the horizon lengthening the shadows of the pines, which appeared to emerge from the graves like specters fleeing their sepulchers, in an unprecedented rebellion against Death. Startled, I hurried up to return to the hamlet, turning often toward the cemetery, being afraid some ghost pursued me. In the dying luminosity of dusk the shapes of the trees got confusing, and I seemed to discover fantastic animals and human figures lurking behind the trunks. At the height of my delirium, I got a foot stuck among the dried branches of a fallen Holm oak; out of my mind, I imagined them as hands of dead people that sprouting from the earth tried to catch me. A shudder coursed through my body making my skin stand on end, and dominated by fear I started running terrified, jumping over stones and bushes until arriving exhausted at the settlement. In the distance, after a voluptuous twilight which dyed the clouds blush, the sky painted in indigo, and the stars began to shine.

He resembled a skeleton with the skin glued to the bones; sometimes he moved his arms and legs feebly, so flaccid that he dragged them with difficulty on the sheets. Although he was four years old he appeared to be less than two. Severely malnourished and dehydrated, he lay face upward lacking strength to get up. His black eyes, languid and sad, looked at me without seeing me; rather, his fixed look got lost in the void. When we injected him, he only grimaced in pain; he tried to scream but he hardly managed to open his parched mouth, he had the tongue adhered to the gums; he could no longer cry. He was like one of those moribund children from the famines in Africa; those who appear on television and seem to live in an imaginary world, distant, unreal. He was burning with fever and we could never give him an intravenous drip, his veins were collapsed. He had been suffering from diarrhea and vomit for fifteen days. In the beginning he was treated by a young health promoter from a remote community; deficiently prepared, she made a wrong diagnosis and the problem got worse. Afterwards they took him to a quack so that she *"raised his soft spot,"* but, however much the woman pushed his palate with her fingers, she didn't manage to raise it. Now it was too late, the child died at two o'clock in the morning. The mother, a tarahumara young woman with worn out, filthy clothes, remained all the time in a corner, squatted and silent. Every now and then she turned and, on seeing us sticking the needles into the lean flesh of the little kid, she made a grimace of displeasure and compassion. When we informed her about the death, she stood there for a moment contemplating the immobile body, then she wiped away two small tears and without saying a word she wrapped him up in his dirty blankets. She went out into the night filled with mysterious murmurs, and with her dead son in her arms she disappeared into the darkness, bound for the distant sierras.

The high rate of infant mortality is very patent in the indigenous communities of the Tarahumara, even though owing to the remoteness and inaccessibility of the region there are no reliable statistics. The problem is not, however, different from the one faced by other autochthonous groups of the country or, even, the inhabitants of many destitute neighborhoods that emerge on the suburbs of the big cities. Nonetheless, taking advantage of the chronicity of the problem, the yellow press publishes it periodically as news, giving it an apocalyptic overtone, making the forgetful ones get a guilty conscience and causing a social commotion that obligates the health institutions to implement extraordinary programs to solve *"the emergency,"* which rarely reach the most marginalized and needy areas. In one of such *"contingencies,"* a nonprofit organization conducted a supposed fundraising for charity that received disproportionate advertising; in the end, only a few sacks of potatoes and beans arrived to the affected zones, inedible because they were already germinated and full of weevils; the beneficiaries were the goats. The local governor, disappointed and upset, recalled the incident: *"they saw us with face of pigs."* Unfortunately, these publicized campaigns have provoked the envy of some mestizos who imagine the tarahumaras enjoying the goodness of charity. One of their comments is illustrative: *"they're just making that bunch of freeloaders lazier."*

The truth is that these *"outbreaks"* of humanism do not provide a real solution to the core causes and all comes to nothing; the tarahumaran children keep on dying. The macabre irony is that this mortality, as a way of regulating the population, governed by natural selection, is one of the factors that have allowed the subsistence of the rarámuris as an independent ethnic group, composed of the individuals the most capable to overcome the adversities of their environment. Given the fecundity of the tarahumara women and the poverty of the lands where they have been cornered, if all the children that are born managed to survive, a grave demographic explosion would have occurred in the sierra since a long time ago, seriously affecting the environment as the scarce natural resources would be depleted in a short period. The precarious situation of the Indian would worsen rapidly, suffering famines and an intolerable deterioration of his living conditions, which would drive him to a mass exodus in search of a more promising future, dealing a mortal blow to the existence of this aboriginal group as such. In fact this phenomenon is already arising at present, to a slower rhythm though.

One of the most discouraging and disconcerting experiences for health workers is facing the apparent negligence of the relatives in caring for the sick and the application of treatment. Frequently the uncertainty that medicaments are administered correctly remains because, due to ancestral practices, it is a common tendency to consider them magic potions from which a single dose sufficed to be relieved. This makes extremely difficult the fight against contagious diseases like tuberculosis, endemic in the region, which require prolonged treatments and the sanitary control of the sick; an almost impossible task for the continuous movement of the population and the maddening custom of changing their name; odd custom that completely disrupts the monitoring of medical records.

In some large families, whose economic conditions are always critical, a particularly disturbing situation arises. When the younger children fall ill, the tendency to neglect their treatment is very manifest, giving the troubling impression that their death would be acceptable to reduce the burden on their meager provisions and better satisfy the family needs. This kind of behavior, perhaps a reflection of a compassionate desire to prevent children from suffering, has been well documented in various ancient social groups; even though from the limited perspective of modern man it would seem horrific and barbarous, it could have deep millenary roots and would be a

natural way of birth control admissible for a society that lives immersed in Nature and is ruled by its laws. Death would be the impregnable bastion where life defends itself.

It took me years to acknowledge this, which for many health workers and inhabitants of the sierra is something clear and unquestionable, and even considered as a cultural trait. The anecdotes the social workers could tell on this topic are innumerable. An extreme case took place in a remote hamlet, with a tarahumara who constantly got his wife pregnant; shortly after the babies were born, they died in mysterious accidents during the drinking bouts of the father. The series of deaths in implausible circumstances aroused the suspicions of the health promoters assigned to the community, who, irate, made the woman confess the infanticides of her husband. When I asked them why they didn't report him to the police, they replied frustrated: *"they don't do anything to them; they already know that's the way it goes amongst themselves."* Discussing the problem with a couple of tarahumara teachers exceptionally prepared and interested in their culture, they conceded an indisputable lack of care in attending the patients, but they attributed it to the ignorance of the parents, who did not acknowledge the necessity of providing special care to the sick children, treating them just the same as healthy children, with the consequent fatal results. When I used these arguments to refute a health promoter with several years of service in the sierra and a sincere commitment to the welfare of the Indians, she responded to me, categorical: *"it's not true, they let them die."*

Many times it is the patient himself who neglects his treatment. On the days prior to the celebrations of Holy Week, a young man who was going to participate as Pharisee suffered an extensive burn on an arm; in spite of our recommendations, he neither came to have his wound dressed, nor did he *"avoid sunning himself,"* refusing to take the medicines in order to be able to drink tesgüino. Three days later he returned burning with fever, with the wound covered with a purulent skin and a monstrous swelling of the arm; we had to force him to be injected at the clinic to prevent an amputation. Amongst the most dramatic cases is the one of a peasant with a foot affected with gangrene. Firmly resolved to be attended by a neighboring health promoter, who in the past had cured him of a minor injury, he refused to sell some sheep to be able to transport him to the city; the amputation of the foot was inevitable. Exasperated for the intransigency of the tarahumara and sick of the nauseating smell that invaded the room where she lodged him, the health promoter ended up not providing the useless treatment to oblige him to go to a hospital. It was in vain, the patient died when the infection *"spread"* to his blood; until the last moment he refused to sell his animals. He was interred at the border of a parched pastureland on which his flock still grazes.

On the opposite side is a growing number of Indians who willingly seek medical services. They are, in general, health promoters or their relatives and acquaintances who have experienced the unquestionable effectiveness and the benefits of modern medicine. Countless times one

has gone to see sick people whose relatives have walked for hours to request a consultation. A typical example was that of Reyes, a tarahumara health promoter from the zone of the canyons. Whenever I visited him he expounded to me, discouraged, the difficulties he had to complete the treatments. He frequently argued with his neighbors because they would not ask for help until their sick relatives got worse, and they became convinced that the offerings of cattle or goats, immolated to appease the anger of the malevolent beings that were harming them, would have no effect. *"That's no good; they're just cheating them so they give them food,"* he criticized the sorcerers, concluding that what they had spent in animals would have better served to go to a hospital, *"but they do not understand."* Nevertheless, in spite of his convictions and confidence in the advantages of modern medicine, ancestral beliefs inculcated in childhood persisted in him. When I told him about an old peyote *"rasper,"* very sick, who was taken by a priest to be hospitalized in Chihuahua, he burst out laughing and said, sarcastically: *"don't they say those ones are very good, why he didn't cure himself?"* Interceding for the old man, I explained to him that the peyote did not cure that disease; then, even though he didn't even know this plant, he lowered his voice and said in a precautionary tone: *"that's not something to get into, that's evil thing."*

Of course there is no lack of abuses and droll situations. A tarahumara young woman with a reputation for being especially promiscuous, went regularly to get contraceptive pills in a rural clinic. Apparently they had been a fabulous discovery for her, almost a revelation, which gave her enormous advantages because they allowed her to have sexual relations without getting worried about becoming pregnant. In one of her appointments to pick up the hormonal contraceptives, she was attended by an adolescent social worker, single and without active sexual life; unexpectedly the Indian asked her out of curiosity if she used them; embarrassed, the young lady only managed to stammer that she was not married and it was not correct for her to take them. Astonished at someone who did not take advantage of the goodness of the medicament, the tarahumara made a face of surprise and replied with a total lack of consideration: *"why not, if it feels so good and with these pills they don't get you knocked up."*

Another important factor that conditions the health problems in the sierra is the insufficient coverage of the sanitary programs, caused by the limited resources and the isolation and inaccessibility of the communities; based on charity, they are characterized by their large deficiencies and their inefficiency owing to the shortage of qualified staff. The majority of the medical posts are occupied by medical students in their social service year or recent graduates with little experience. For the paramedical positions people with minimal studies, and swiftly trained in deficient courses, are hired. Unfortunately, they are the only ones who out of necessity accept to work under the rigors that impose a geographical environment and a social organization very different from one's own. Salaries are so derisory that one spends almost a half of it just to get out of the communities. There is besides the distressing perspective of a mediocre professional future, isolated from the continual and amazing advances of medical science. The doctor of a Jesuit hospital put it in a harsh and categorical manner: *"here you come to gather dust; now, it surely is a fact that only crazy or drunk one bears to stay."*

Insecurity is another serious problem. Several physicians have died in aviation accidents or murdered by shooting in the violent communities where drug trafficking rules. The case of an ambulance which was assaulted in the middle of the sierra is illustrative; after despoiling them of the little money they carried, the thieves forced the doctor, the driver and the relative of the patient to get him out along with the stretcher, and they fled with the vehicle abandoning them on the road, exposed to the bitter winter cold. It didn't help to beseech they allowed them to take the sick man to a hospital because he was seriously ill. The driver had to walk four hours in the night to get aid, while the doctor and the relative took care of the patient.

The principal consequence of so many difficulties is a constant turnover of personnel, which affects the continuity of the health programs. Frequently the posts remain vacant during months. Unfortunately, the current health system has favored an absurd devaluation and corruption of the medical services, fomenting the indiscriminate use of medicaments. The altruistic sense of the first researchers, who sought to mitigate the ailments of humanity, has been also lost and nobody marvels anymore at the prodigy of being able to cure, with a minute pill, diseases that just a few decades ago were deadly.

On a hot summer day, sitting at the edge of a pastureland full of ridges and furrows, which served as a landing strip, I talked with the doctor of an isolated medical unit, located on a narrow plateau between two formidable canyons. We were waiting for the arrival of the airplane that would come for him after fetching other doctors commissioned in clinics situated even farther away into the sierra. The appointment was concerted through the radio of the place. Air traveling was the only practical way of going out and, in spite of the risk, all preferred to fly an hour to walk several days going up and down slopes to arrive at the city. Moved by the hope that he would soon meet again with his family after months of separation, he constantly became lost in thought, losing the thread of the conversation. When the frail light aircraft finally landed bouncing on the grass, he left running to board it. From the window, the pilot threw to the ground a couple of bundles *"for the school,"* and immediately got ready to leave; neither did he want to stay a long time, for he was more worried about the difficulties of the takeoff than knowing the exoticness of the tarahumaras. With hair-raising boldness the aircraft gained height heavily on a short length of the strip, raising a dense dust cloud, sinking then into the abyss, turned into a fulgurant point that purred in the immensity of the canyons. While I observed how it flew away, I recalled the last comments of the physician, where his frustration on facing a totally unknown culture was reflected. With an exasperation verging on comicality, he ranted and raved about the indigenous customs making furious gestures: *"how can they be amongst so much filth; they have a mess of junk all over the place. What's the trouble of tidying up their houses to live better?"* And he concluded categorically: *"if I had to clean one of those huts I would leave nothing, they are mere stinking rags; I'm certain I would burn it all!"*

In the pre-Columbian era, living in the relative isolation of their distant territories, the Indians managed to harmonize their simple existence with the environment, maintaining a stable and rather healthy population. Herbal medicine, with its multiple resources, was enough to overcome the ailments of a highly resistant people, well adapted to the conditions of the place. The arrival of the Spaniards caused a hecatomb, unbalancing this subtle relationship, which has gotten worse nowadays, owing to the constant migrations of the tarahumaras. In spite of the goodwill of the local shamans, herbal remedies have little usefulness against the respiratory, gastrointestinal and tuberculous infections which cause serious damage to their communities, due to the unwholesomeness, malnutrition and overcrowded conditions they live in.

I remember a strange and fascinating anecdote from a teacher of the faculty of medicine, who told us about an old professor of his who had performed his social service year in the Tarahumara. After living several months with the natives, he discovered, intrigued, that they were in the habit of storing hard tortillas under a petate in the dampest and darkest corners of their dwellings, which ended up all covered with fungi in vivid colors. When a member of the family got sick of cough or diarrhea they made him eat a piece of these tortillas and, mysteriously, he got cured. Although he was very impressed, he didn't study such a remarkable find in depth. A short time later doctor Fleming discovered penicillin, produced by fungi, and the professor was left frustrated for the rest of his life; he had lost the unique opportunity of discovering the antibiotics. The moral was that one should always try to apply the scientific method to research diseases. After long years in quest, I have not managed to find the *"miraculous"* tortillas. If they were ever used, it's very probable this knowledge has been forgotten like so many others acquired with the effort of countless generations.

When I have invited indigenous medicine men to see patients together with me, they have invariably contributed something to the prescriptions; be it a simple brew or an aromatic ointment. With the passage of time, reflecting on the implications of that school account, a more transcendental meaning has been disclosed which, for its simpleness, today seems obvious. I wonder if,

disdaining the wisdom of traditional medicine, amassed for centuries, we are throwing away a knowledge that has allowed man to live in harmony with Nature, and which could teach us more natural and safe methods, and maybe even take a new approach to our way of solving health problems.

Ventura was twenty-five years old when a huge *"trunker"* truck knocked him down, shattering his *"haunch"* in five pieces. Fortunately, the bishop of the Tarahumara of that time, a most beloved and respected priest in the region, was visiting the place; he got an intrepid pilot to land on a rustic strip close to Ventura's house, to transport him by plane to Chihuahua; the bishop himself accompanied him to the hospital. *"I survived by a sheer miracle,"* he acknowledged gratefully. *"Ev'r since the accident I'm bad fo' walking,"* he said in a tone of tranquil resignation while he advanced slowly, slightly training his left leg; his voluminous barrel thorax rocked with difficulty on his narrow and deformed hip, which barely seemed to have room for his thin legs. We crossed the forest in the evening on our way to his house, when we came across the dirt strip; more than thirty years had passed and even pine trees had grown in the middle of it. A long time ago the army closed it because it was not registered and they were afraid it would be used by drug traffickers. Curious, I asked him what would happen if today, three decades later, a similar emergency came up; shaking his head he replied without hesitation: *"it wud be wurs."* He would have to be transported by land on foot or in a *"troc,"* *"if you're lucky to get one"*; several hours would elapse before arriving where he could be treated properly. *"I wud surely die."*

𝕿*here come the spotty ones!* shouted excited the bunch of kids, and off they went in a mad rush to meet the tarahumara dancers who, from all the surrounding settlements, came to the village to celebrate Holy Week. They were just the first participants; those who lived in the farthest communities would arrive till the following day, after a journey of almost two days walking through the anfractuous sierras. They came in groups composed of two long files headed by a standard bearer, who carried a white standard with the image of Jesus Christ and the name of their locality. He was the captain and directed the dances brandishing his flag vigorously, drawing crosses in the air. Their strange attires were impressive; almost bare, their only clothing was the traditional triangular loose skirt made of a rough cotton cloth, called zapeta, which came down to their knees and was tied to their waist with a wide cloth band in vivid colors, which formed a droll bundle on their back, because in it they wrapped their everyday clothes to change when the festivities were over. Tied to their neck they wore a multicolored large handkerchief, and many crowned their heads with elegant panaches, deftly elaborated with black turkey feathers. The attire was complemented by the typical huaraches and a long wooden stick, decorated with multicolored geometric designs, which was intended to be a sword and served as a walking stick during the dances. They had their face painted in white with a special kind of mud, reserved for such occasion, that they also applied with the fingertips on their torso and limbs, to adorn them with white dots; that was why they called them *"the spotty ones,"* and they represented the Pharisees, personifying evil.

A couple of musicians marched in the rear of each group, measuring the cadence with the rhythmic beating of their drums, accompanying them at regular intervals with the shrill notes of reed flutes, which they carried tied to the edge of the drums to be able to play them without requiring use of their hands. The tremendous display of energy was admirable; the dancers jumped and turned in the air, then ran in a circle following the flag bearer, and they formed again in files. When several adjacent groups danced at the same time, they caused a real muddle; looking at the exalted multitude moving in all directions, as possessed by a sudden collective madness, I didn't understand how they managed to follow the rhythm in that confusion of sounds. Contemplating from the door of his small shop the apparent disorder, a robust rancher with a thick mustache, born in the place and accustomed from his childhood to speak tarahumara, commented to me with a strong sierran accent: *"I've never grasped these fiestas; you just see loads of Indians turning and turning, now they go up the hill, now they go down to the river; it's a devil of a jumble.''* In reality, it was not that complicated; on one side of the church door was the program of dances, processions and religious ceremonies that the festivity comprised, and carefully studying the dances, a simple routine of movements was patent. Nevertheless, for the children it was not that easy to learn it and they constantly made mistakes, missing the step, turning in the opposite direction or colliding with their companions as they missed the sequence, provoking their own laughter and the others'. But, although for the kids many things were tolerated and they could even quit the dances if they got tired, for the older ones the commitment was very formal; anyone who decided to participate in the celebration was obliged to finish it, and since, besides the exhausting effort, it required an expense for clothing, the participants had to give it serious consideration before engaging themselves in it.

Only men took part in the dances and there was no age limit; youngsters under ten years of age and men already old participated alike. The presence of light-skinned dancers called much my attention, and I supposed they were mestizos; soon I learned some of them surely were and were paying promised offerings, nonetheless, the majority were authentic tarahumaras...but blonds! Women arrived after the groups of dancers. They came dressed with kerchiefs tied to their head, loose-fitting blouses and fluffy skirts of several layers, which bounced on their hips as they walked; in spite of the intense color of their clothing, they demonstrated a splendid taste to combine them. Shyly they congregated against the walls of the shelter-school, which framed the parvis of the church, and discreetly observed the dances, sitting very close together on the ground, wrapped up in their long shawls, forming a variegated group of immobile figures, with a bunch of kids *"huddled"* around them.

One of the flag bearers seemed to have a relevant position because instead of directing the dances he was always beside the governor and his officials. Definitely he was not tarahumara; even though he wore huaraches and a cloth band on his long hair, his features denounced him, above all his sturdy and distinguished personality stood out; tall and slender, he dressed a suit without necktie and had a refined bearing, very moderate in his acts. A simple question to the residents of the village was enough to find out his story in full detail. He was a former Jesuit who for a long time had been priest of the place, until the rumors about a hidden love affair with a tarahumara woman who helped him doing the church chores began. To hold the scandal back, the bishop had to come to *"uncover the secret,"* which was on everybody's mouth, forcing the priest to choose between priesthood and the woman. It didn't take long for him to decide to abandon the habit and to go live with his wife in a modest house in the sierra, like any other tarahumara. By common consent of the community, and in virtue of the services he had rendered to the Indians, he was appointed First Flag Bearer.

Before beginning the celebrations of Holy Week a simple ceremony of yúmari had been performed, which was intended to invoke the goodwill of the gods. In the parvis, in front of the door of the church, a little table covered with a white tablecloth was placed, putting offerings of tesgüino and food on both ends; to one side they thrust three wooden crosses in the ground. An old man who *"knew how to communicate with Onorúame"* conducted the ritual, dancing slowly before the altar, making short back and forth movements, accompanied by several women who formed in a row by his side and walked following his steps. He shook rhythmically a rattle with the intention of apprising the gods and breaking their apathy to encourage them to accept their presents; at the same time, he intoned with a deep voice a monotonous and sad chant, so expressive, it resembled more a supplicant lament. From time to time he stopped to rest and drank a little of tesgüino from the offering, sharing with the rest of the participants. They continued this way until dusk, when the Pharisee lit large bonfires on the rocky prominences of the hills surrounding the village. Holy Week began *"searching for God"*; the bonfires represented torches and were a remembrance of the search and arrest of Jesus Christ in the Garden, after the betrayal of Judas.

Two whole days of intense activity followed, in which the mestizos of the place and the Jesuit priests of the local mission, who said masses assisted by the tarahumara leaders and the nuns in charge of the shelter-school, also participated. The processions congregated the whole village, cramming the narrow and stony back streets. The multitude advanced slowly, preceded by the tireless Pharisee dancers, carrying on a portable platform a coarse statue of Jesus Christ that, with inexpressive face, bore on his shoulder a small wooden cross. The Virgin Mary dressed with a purple cloak came behind, softly rocking and staring at the crowd with her fixed eyes wide open. The cortege followed a path marked with wooden crosses thrust in the ground next to slender arches made of intertwined branches of pine, under which the images had to pass, stopping for a moment to say a prayer in silence, the men uncovering their heads. At the sudden resounding of the drums the march and the impetuous waving of the flags resumed. The final procession was to the cemetery, located in the outskirts of the village, to celebrate the *"Holy Burial"*; two indigenous officers carried on their shoulders the figure of Jesus Christ wrapped in a petate which hung from a thick pole, tied from its ends. The golden light of the late afternoon made the tangle of parched weeds grown between the tombs stand out, which swayed in the wind, emitting beautiful sparkles of gold. Mounted on the rocks of an adjacent hill, a part of the crowd observed the bizarre retinue make a turn inside the graveyard, staying for a long while in the center, addressing a solemn prayer to God, and then returning to the church amidst a loud racket.

The dances of the Pharisee lasted a good part of the day, being interrupted only to eat or bring the firewood that would fuel the night bonfires; in the evening their intensity increased, participating a growing number of dancers. At night the spectacle was unbelievable, like a dream

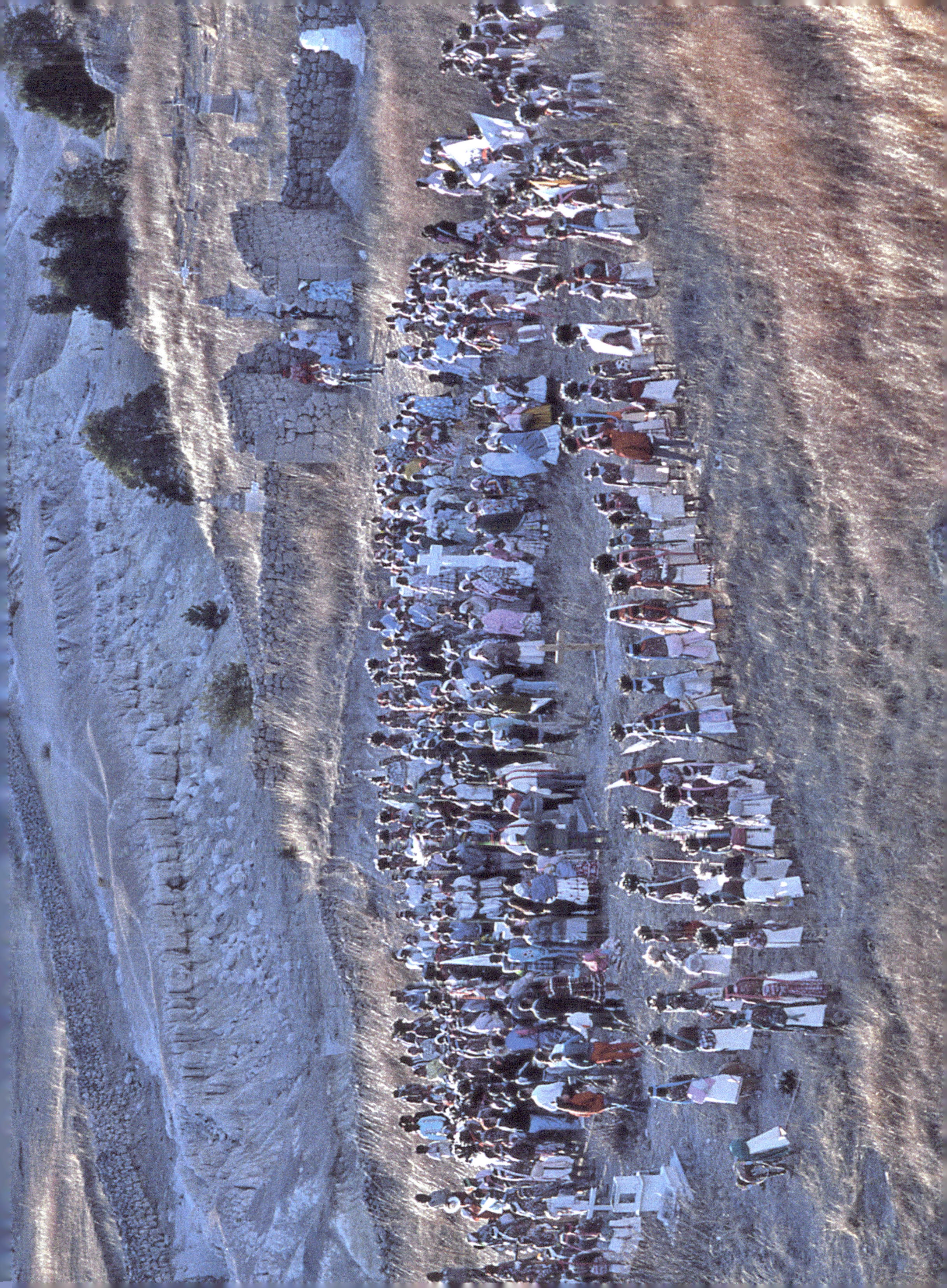

that had taken us back in time, to the most primitive stages of human culture. Under a jet-black sky spangled with stars, enormous bonfires illuminated the parvis and the broad open space in front of the shelter-school; the groups of dancers gathered around them to rest and protect themselves from the intense cold, warming alternately the chest and the back, like chickens being roasted. Suddenly a chaotic frenzy unleashed and all the Pharisees started dancing synchronized, raising dense clouds of dust. The sound of the drums and flutes became deafening, reverberating on the walls and the nearby hills, producing a flow of scrambled echoes that seemed to come from other times. The light of the fire projected gigantic feathered shadows on the walls, which repeated the feverish movements of the dancers, resembling gargantuan phantoms driven insane by the din of the music. In the last soirée *"the Judas"* appeared, shaking violently on the shoulders of a Pharisee who hurriedly followed a musician; to the rhythm of a drum and a flute they traversed the open space in an exhausting race, dancing brief moments with each group. The dummy, life-size and stuffed with straw, was dressed like a mestizo, with cowboy boots and a tilted hat. Through the open fly, a big wooden penis emerged, provoking the laughter of the public who shouted dirty words at him reproving his cheek; he was the living personification of evil and indecency, and he seemed a just reproach against several mestizos of the locality who, inebriated, danced grotesquely between the files of the Pharisees, mimicking the dances in mockery, trying to capture the attention, and despising the sacred meaning of the festivity.

The celebrations ended on Holy Saturday. That day, very early, they began to share out the tesgüino among the participants; then *"the pascola"* started, an exotic dance performed by two dancers who differentiated from the Pharisees because they had the body profusely decorated with little lines and dots, meticulously drawn in white, black and ocher colors. In time to a violin and a drum, they danced describing tight circles, taking short and dragged steps, tamping in the earth tiny stones that a young man threw under their feet. After dancing in front of the shelter-school they crossed the open space and went into the parvis surrounded by the crowd which formed a wide corridor, at the end of which was the Judas, leaned against the wall of the church. The pascoleros had the commission of destroying evil; they danced a while under the crude belfry that stood at a corner of the parvis and, followed by their musicians, they approached winding the dummy, beating it and throwing stones at it, while the crowd, amused, cheered them on by shouting and guffawing. By that time many tarahumaras were already drunk. When the dancers moved away, the First Flag Bearer approached the Judas making movements in the shape of a cross with his flag to conjure it away, at the same time his guards stuck it with their spears and the crowd rushed on it kicking it, spitting at it and pulling its legs and arms to tear it into pieces; dirty and ripped up, it was left lying on the ground, with its huge wooden penis pointing to the firmament.

Since dawn the weather had changed abruptly; unexpectedly, dark storm clouds covered the sky announcing a snowfall as a cold epilogue for the passion of the Christ. Nonetheless it was the third day of exhausting festivities, the dancers continued dancing bravely in spite of the icy wind which made their seminude bodies shiver. Their tenacity was amazing, submitting themselves most fervently to a corporeal sacrifice that emulated the Calvary of the Son of God. The tarahumaras kept on *"protecting God"* so that the Devil would not harm him while he recovered from this difficult critical moment. In their weary expression they seemed to harbor the secret hope that their earthly suffering would make them deserve the supreme good promised in the Holy Scripture, in one of the most beautiful and poetic moments of Christianity: when Jesus Christ, after dying crucified, rose from the dead to ascend to Heaven and reach eternal life; immune to pain, to the human evil, to Death...

Not in all the tarahumara communities the ceremonies of Holy Week are as rigorous and formal; although they have many similarities, they are usually simpler and more spontaneous in the isolated villages where the indigenous leaders organize them without the participation of church ministers. In a remote hamlet in the bottom of the canyons, the local governor headed the celebrations pronouncing a sermon standing beside the door of the rustic church of adobe; very straight and rigid, with the arms folded on his chest, he spoke in a low voice and with great rapidity, without making inflections of the voice, which was hardly heard at the limits of the parvis. He had his eyes fixed ahead, over the panaches of the Pharisee dancers who, lined up in front of the temple, wore multicolored loose shirts and had the body covered in reddish mud. These ones appeared not to be paying attention, and they got distracted playing with their feet or looking in the distance. Behind them were the women, who sat on the ground looking downward, forming a compact and still group; the children played, carefree, around them. Unexpectedly a dog got among the dancers, who began to kick it and beat it with their *"swords,"* shouting and laughing while the animal ran, frightened, from one line to another howling pitifully; when it managed to get out of the parvis, it ran away at top speed towards the hill. During the incident the governor had continued speaking as if nothing were happening, indifferent to the multitude; his brown face, tanned by the sun, had a serious expression, and he gave the impression of repeating, just for himself, a speech learned by heart. To finish and, apparently, with the intention that the few mestizos who visited the place also understood, he said in a solemn tone in Spanish: *"have respect for God; don't be shitting behind the church."*

Here the fiesta followed a very peculiar pattern; the community only congregated in the church for short periods to perform the ceremonies that the irregular program comprised. The rest of the time they dispersed in several groups and spent the time visiting the houses scattered on the steep slopes of the canyon, where women prepared beans, ground corn to make tortillas and kept a watchful eye on the enormous clay pots in which the tesgüino fermented. The guests arrived in file led by a musician who played a drum and a flute at the same time. They congregated around the pots to talk and drink sitting on the stones or on the ground, under the shade of the trees; a few of them started to dance disorderly making circles in front of three wooden crosses thrust into the ground next to the vessels. A little group of musicians played out of tune chords on a violin and a guitar, hardly following the time of a drum and a flute, while the main dancer, affected by alcohol, tapped his feet clumsily trying to follow the rhythm with the clusters of rattles he carried tied to his ankles. After consuming the tesgüino of a pot, they restarted their pilgrimage going to another house, on the opposite slope. The majority had begun to drink before the celebrations commenced; by the start of the yúmari many participants were already drunk, and on beginning the dances of Pharisees in front of the church or in the short processions around the shelter-school, almost all advanced staggering. At night the rounds went on, and only the drums crossing at intervals from one slope to the other could be heard. Their ability to guide themselves in the darkness through the steep and entangled trails was amazing, as they were completely inebriated and without lights to illuminate the way.

An important ceremony in the temple was planned for the afternoon of the last day of the festivity; the man in charge arrived punctually to open the door and arrange the austere interior whose only adornment was a long band of Greek frets in red ocher color painted on the base of the walls. We waited in vain for more than an hour, sitting on the wall that delimited the parvis; suddenly, the *"sacristan"* leapt to his feet and went to lock the church, concluding naturally: *"they did no longer come."* On the way back to his house we found a dancer lying at the edge of the trail; drunk to the point of unconsciousness, he snored loudly and his multicolored clothes were all muddy. Next to him a woman remained sitting in abnegation, immobile and silent; she was his wife. A little further on we found other dancers sleeping on the ground; a dog licked their lips hurriedly to eat the dried remnants of tesgüino. While we passed jumping over them, the tarahumara said with simplicity: *"they're going to have to skip this dancing fo' finishing the fiesta on time."* Perplexed and amused at the same time, I couldn't help smiling; such a detachment from the religious formalities was unexpected. I didn't manage to define that attitude; first I was tempted to consider it as a palpable token of their high esteem for the individual independence, but on looking that pile of stultified men, trapped by the alcohol, my romantic notion of witnessing their idealistic conception of liberty vanished. Simply, like in any human society, they seemed to give priority to mundane pleasures over heavenly commitments.

Close to the evening two kids came running to ask me to go see an injured person. They were so agitated they only babbled incoherent words, mixing Spanish and Rarámuri, without managing to explain to me what had happened. We went hastily up the steep slope until reaching, panting, a small terrace high up on the canyon. In a narrow room with badly built stone walls was lying on a petate a half asleep adolescent. By his side a mature woman, tall and stout, rather obese, tried to revive him lavishing him with affection; she was the grandmother. It had been a mere brawl of drunkards; being amidst the bunch, they just dealt him a light blow to the nape, but, dulled by liquor, the boy fell to the ground and, seized by hysteria, he burst into tears like a child; alarmed, his relatives took him quickly to his house. After clearing the crowd that thronged in front of the door, because *"they were taking the air away from him,"* I gave him some tablets *"to reduce the inflammation of the blows"*; then I asked for a little water to apply moist compresses before rubbing him with a salve. Solicitous, the woman brought a small bucket and, kneeling down next to me, she said with an emphatic tone of a good connoisseur: *"it is cool, to bring the heat down."*

Minutes later, revitalized by the pampering and the massages, the young man smiled again and everybody bantered with him, giving him affectionate pats on the back. We went out into the yard where, once they got over their fright, the people chatted cheerfully and the musicians began to play a violin, accompanying it with flutes and drums. To celebrate, the family incited the grandmother to dance but, inhibited by embarrassment, at first she refused; when her grandson invited her formally holding out his arm to her, she made a childish gesture of rejection and burst into boisterous laughter; then, relieved from the worry, they took each other by the hand and started dancing in a circle. I remained enraptured looking at that enormous matrona jumping and turning in the air with the agility of a little girl; her loose multicolored clothes flapped in the wind and her face, rubicund due to the effort, irradiated a beautiful happiness. Euphoric and grateful, she asked the boy to give me his panache of Pharisee as a present, and they continued dancing until the moon peered over the edge of the immense canyon.

Chapter V – **THOSE MULTIFACETED NEIGHBORS**

a) – With Time on Your Back

Doña Eustolia was the kind of person in whom time seemed to have stopped; as if, tired of its interminable fleeing, it would have fallen asleep for an instant. Among the fine features of her wrinkled face, the vivacious look of her blue eyes stood out. She must have been very beautiful in her youth. In spite of her advanced age, she attended very carefully her small general store, located in an isolated village which marked the confines of the lands inhabited by the mestizos; a little further on, where the geography became more inhospitable and inaccessible, the rarámuri territory began. Customers were scarce because the majority of the houses were abandoned; many of the residents had emigrated to the city or the neighboring towns to improve their living conditions. Some of them had gone to the United States as *"wetbacks."* That was why those who bought from her the most were the Indians, who came to stock up with provisions from their distant hamlets, to several hours of walking distance upstream. But, although it was the only store within a radius of tens of kilometers, it didn't prosper as the sons of the lady wished, because the canons of civilized commerce vanished in this isolated zone of transition, where things returned to their natural course and people were still ruled by the archaic system of bartering, which doña Eustolia accepted without a qualm. Once a tarahumara old man arrived laden with an enormous bale of stubble, and traded it to her for flour, beans, candles, straps for his huaraches and a soda, as a bonus, *"for the weariness."*

I always stop for a moment to talk with her; her pleasant stories that invariably go back to her childhood, and light up her face with joy, captivate me. Her father and her husband were free-lance gold diggers in a nearby mine. She was widowed a long time ago; she lives in a picturesque little house of adobe surrounded by flowers, located in front of her shop, in which she treasures all her keepsakes. She says she lives at ease in the place, *"it is very peaceful"*; besides she could have her flowerpots, hens and pigs without disturbing anybody, and didn't lack anything to eat. Only at times she complained about how problematic it was to transport the merchandise on droves of mules through the narrow and stony trails; they had to wade the river several times and in the rainy season it became dangerous. She had as an assistant a tarahumara old man who accompanied her all the time. When she agreed to let me take a photograph of her, the first thing she did was to call the rarámuri to stand by her side, who timidly refused while he hurriedly spruced his long hair up, trying to arrange the cloth band that adorned his head; with imprudence I asked her jokingly if she had already married again, and she answered very upset: *"no sir, one has already had one's husband; here it is not like in the city, that every other minute they get married and unmarried. They even seem like little animals."*

One of the most disconcerting peculiarities of the sierra is the possibility of an unexpected encounter with blond people who live isolated in remote communities. These features, of European origin, are part of the heritage the Spaniards left during the Colony, when they penetrated into those remote places in search of fortune. But they weren't the only ones who left a trace; in the epoch of the French invasion to the country, Gallic and Belgian troops fought in this region and suffered serious defeats that made the soldiers flee in disorder, taking shelter in hidden and distant spots; as time passed, they ended up joining with mestizo and even indigenous women. Today, in an incredible paradox of fate, it is surprising to find in the humble tarahumara homes fair-skinned people with light colored eyes who, though they seem foreigners, only speak in rarámuri, are dressed in their traditional style and live completely immersed in their culture.

But the past does not only remain in the physiognomy of people. Besides the many uses and wont, on comparing the language of the old colonial narrations of laypeople and religious with the current way of talking in the remote villages of the Tarahumara, it is interesting to discover that many expressions of common usage are similar in spite of the time elapsed. Words like truje (brought), híbanos (went), mesmamente (just), recebir (receive) and others, that in the cities are considered as proofs of the ignorance of a person, are, in reality, simple testimonies of the persistence of ancient Spanish, because in these isolated places language does not evolve with the same rapidity as in the large urban areas.

A curious and reveling idiom of the tarahumaras on speaking *"the Castile"*, is the omission of the pronoun *"usted"* as a courtesy treatment, addressing all the people without distinction using the familiar *"tú"* form; but they don't do it with the purpose of insulting or being disrespectful; simply, not being Spanish their mother tongue, this reflects their incomprehension of grammatical forms and social formalities which are completely strange to them. Nevertheless, on these grounds many mestizos justify themselves to brand them *"sassy"* or fools and ignorant, dissimulating with insolence their own incapability to learn Rarámuri. It is remarkable that the majority of the aborigines have enough command of Spanish to communicate with us, who, considering ourselves smarter and more intelligent, just barely manage to babble some phrases in their language; to which, with ridiculous disdain and pedantry, we call dialect.

ominga kept on smoking in spite of the cancer, which had already eaten away at one of her breasts. Faced with the strong opposition of her relatives, she tried to do it secretly, but invariably her children discovered her; she justified herself saying she was quitting it little by little, assuring them she only *"blew one a day."* Nonetheless, in time it was evident she was smoking *"the only cigarette of the day"* at all times. They had extirpated a breast, emptying the contiguous armpit, trying that *"the illness didn't spread."* Besides, they subjected her to radiation and toxic medicaments that made her lose her hair; however, she was pleased, when the hair grew back and was silkier and curly, *"before I had Indian's locks."* She knew she was dying; she lost weight in an alarming way and more and more she felt weaker. Her life was exhausting and she tried to *"make the most of each little piece, as much as I can."*

She was widowed very young. Her husband was killed in a shooting, *"over there in Sinaloa"*; he was a policeman. She had three children with him, but soon after his death one of them drowned in a pond of the river, even though he knew how to swim well enough; *"he plunged into the water and just never came out, they say there is an animal down there, that maybe it ate him."* Years later she had another girl; when I asked if she had married again she answered casually: *"no, just like that; they say the one who does not shack up is not a soldier."* Her relatives got very upset because *"she was just giving flight to the hanging thread,"* and they took the girl away from her for a couple of years, until time brought about the reconciliation. Today, her daughter has been married for a while; her marriage is one of those rare cases in which a mestizo woman gets married with a pureblood Indian. *"He is a liquid tarahumara,"* said Dominga, whose dearest wish was sharing life with her grandson who lived up the street, two houses away from hers. Although she and her children had fair skin and some of them even blond hair, the child looked like a rarámuri for his dark brown complexion, his thick lips and his black and straight hair. With popular wisdom, the lady stated: *"that's because the blood of the Indian is very strong, it dominates."* Fondly she called him *"my little tarahumara,"* and talked to him coddling him, intermingling Spanish with Rarámuri, which she tried to learn to be able to communicate with the kid, to whom his parents were teaching to speak in both languages. Proudly she recounted how, unlike the mestizo children, her grandson hardly ever got sick and endured more the inclemency of the weather, running barefoot in the cold and eating by fistfuls the snow of the fields. Also, being less than two years old, he already knew *"to throw out gobs."* Nevertheless, she had serious problems with her son-in-law because he drank a lot; above all, when his relatives visited him, who consumed the alcohol *"as if water"* till they dropped inebriated; *"they become very stubborn,"* she said angrily. Frequently, he abandoned his job to *"engage in the drunk."* Lamenting it, Dominga passed her time searching for remedies *"to get him rid of the vice."*

To help support the family, her daughter had to get a job as a nurse in an isolated rural clinic. Since then, she could seldom visit her mother; it was very expensive to be *"coming and going"* every other minute, and in winter snowfalls blocked the way. Besides, she struggled much to *"enter"* the village; first she had to find a *"good lift"* on a timber truck and travel three hours by dirt road to a crossroads; from there she had to continue on foot, four more hours, going up and down hills to arrive at the community. Before leaving, she called by radio to the clinic in order to have them go and wait for her at the crossroads with a donkey, to transport the child because he still could not withstand walking so much. Although her husband had gone with her, he often left her alone and returned to the town to go out partying; he only worked at times for short periods. When by chance he came across his mother-in-law on the street, he tried to *"dodge around her"*; if he didn't manage to do it, he went, deceitfully, to greet her, offering her some little gift that she always rejected, scolding him, indignantly: *"get outta here, you fainéant drunkard, you should instead be taking bottles to your son."*

Artemio, the eldest son of Dominga, was one of those young men, frank and obliging, that one often finds in the sierra. Shy and retiring, he was candid enough to confess aboveboard, that at his twenty nine years of age, he had neither had a girlfriend nor did he know anything about women; dealing with them intimidated him. Nonetheless, in his moments of courage he said with conviction: *"who knows, maybe any of these days I get married."* But, for the time being, he was more fascinated with an extravagant wrist watch he recently had bought *"in the siti,"* whose novelty was that on pressing a button a sensual feminine little voice was activated which told the time. He tried to make it noticeable, and his greatest joy was seeing the amazement of those who asked him the time, when he brought the loudspeaker closer to their ears. To help his mother, he elaborated drums which he then sold in the nearby tourist centers as if they were indigenous handcrafts. He had learned to make them copying the rarámuris, to whom he bought the leathers and the wooden frames. Justifying himself, he explained to me that the tarahumaras were not interested in making drums continuously, even less in large quantities and various sizes, *"supposedly it is a lot of trouble to be struggling to sell them; they're only interested in playing them the whole day, they even get you fed up."*

Another of his occupations was breeding hens; with very bad fortune though, because whenever they laid eggs he ate them; *"they are tastier,"* he said cracking a broad smile that inverted his upper lip upwards. Following his mother's advice, he replaced them with eggs that he

bought in the neighboring villages, so that the hen didn't become discouraged. One day several strange eggs appeared in the nest; apparently, the bird found them on the roof and *"gathered them."* But they were old eggs, *"they were dried and stinking,"* said Dominga, whose curiosity led her to break one to inspect it. When the hen saw herself surrounded by so many eggs it decided, to all appearances, that they were already too many and it stopped laying them. One morning, its sole own egg that remained got cracked, a chick with fluffy yellow plumage came out, causing the rejoicing of its owners.

The following day, Artemio accompanied me on a tour around the bordering sierras to show me a spectacular canyon. To the locals it seemed incredible that someone would come only to stroll in the forest and to take photographs; when we returned, the rumor was already spreading that we were looking for plots of land suitable for cultivating drugs. During our absence the chick went out of the nest and fell in a cesspit; it was cheeping for a long time, frightened, while the hen clucked, distressed, going around the hole. Sick as she was, Dominga could not crouch down to rescue it. Gradually the cheeps dwindled, till the chick remained still and silent. As soon as we arrived Artemio went to take it out, but it was already dead. Wanting to console the young man, his mother told him resigned: *"that's'cause it's much too cold; thus young little animals do not resist much, they get frozen stiff right away."*

Dominga would neither survive the winter.

The brilliant light of the gas lamp barely managed to dissipate the darkness that invaded the interior of the little restaurant. In the badly lit corners, diners were vaguely distinguished like ghostly shadows which talked in murmurs; some of them with their hats on. From the kitchen emerged a dense smoke loaded with odors, forming large volutes that ripped the light in shafts while they swirled softly through the air, flooding the whole room. The rustic furnishings revealed, undoubtedly, that it was a typical mestizo village of the bottom of the canyons. It was there where one night they introduced me to the brother Federico. We came across him just on entering, when he prepared to go; he was against the light of the lamp and I didn't manage to look at his face; I could only see his robust silhouette, which had to bend to be able to leave by the door.

Days later we traveled together by *"lift."* We went out of the canyons to take the train. He carried several wooden crates with oranges that he watched very carefully, making sure that nobody sat on them, that they didn't get pounded against the walls. He was going to sell them in the high parts of the sierra to buy an airplane ticket and fly to an isolated hamlet, on the west of the region, to start a new journey. Thus he spent his time, making trips through the Tarahumara. In the middle of the violent shakes of the stake bed truck, that smashed us against the stakes, he told me some of his experiences in pauses. What thrilled him the most was to live with the tarahumaras, and he thanked God for having the chance of sharing their modest lives. He liked to go to the Tubares a lot, following the course of the rivers along the bottom of the canyons; on occasion, he reached way down south of the state of Chihuahua, as far as the zone of Buborígame, where the tepehuanos live. Sometimes his trips got prolonged, and he disappeared from the region for months; nobody knew where he went. He led his drove of mules loaded with merchandise: hoes, lamps, blankets and trinkets that went hanging and clinking on the sides, like carnival adornments. He sold them in the villages he passed *"to finance the journey."* By the light of the day I could observe him fully. He was already a man of mature years, of serene countenance and good manners; he had a large bald patch on his head whose smooth skin gave off sparkles when the sun touched it. Tall and athletic, with a thick silver-haired beard which reached down to half of his chest, his presence was imposing. He seemed a personage escaped from that same Bible he always carried by his side.

Everybody in the region knew the brother Federico; Lico, they called him fondly. He was a Protestant preacher who came to propagate the *"Word of God."* But he didn't do it with the impertinent stubbornness of a fanatic; he preached by example, helping others in whatever he could. Soon the rumor spread that his prayers aided in illness and afflictions; not that they considered him like a saint, no; it was rather as if people believed that his prayers reached higher, and God could listen to them more easily. Such was the faith, that Catholics and pagans invited him, without objection, to pray at their homes to ask for some cause, and he, willingly, spent his evenings and nights praying. Even the nurse at the local health care center said that once she got sick and the medicaments didn't manage to cure her; she only felt improvement when brother Federico went to pray at her house for several days.

Months later, when I returned to the bottom of the canyons, I learned that he had been killed. The circumstances of his death were very confusing and mysterious. Gossip told that a jealous husband shot him in the head when he found him in his house courting his wife; but those who knew him didn't believe it. The event happened in a remote site which took several days of going downstream to reach. There, drug trafficking and violence have established their reign. They *"brot"* his body lying across the back of a mule, with his feet and hands hanging and swinging on the sides, as if they were the trinkets that he sold. He had a hole in the front, from which a trickle of dried blood that stained his face came out. They were starting the transfer when the authorities learned that there were no relatives to claim the cadaver so they decided to return; they buried him right there in a solitary tomb, lost in the immensity of the sierras that he knew so well.

A short time later there was a much-talked-about wedding in the village. A young woman from the place married a young outsider who not long ago had arrived to work there. To their great surprise the locals found out that he was a son of brother Federico. At first, father and son neither knew it, till by chance they conversed. Lico, astonished, considered a miracle the incredible coincidence. As fate would mercifully have it, shortly before his passing, in this remote place, his wish of meeting his offspring again, after almost twenty years of paternal absence, was granted. The mother of the young man and his brothers and sisters attended the wedding. Only then, the village learned that brother Federico was from Sonora, that he had several children and many years ago he had divorced, separating from his family. He had always kept his personal life secret. After the party, his relatives returned to their homeland; none of them went to visit the distant grave.

Several years have elapsed since that, and yesterday a tarahumara told me something that left me astounded. He said that, a few days ago, he saw brother Federico passing near his house, on the slope of a ravine; that he seemed very happy, with his long silver-haired beard, his shining bald patch and his mules loaded with merchandise. Descending slowly along the steep path, he entered the deep gorge that leads to the bottom of the gigantic canyon; as if he were going towards the Tubares...

Chapter VI – **THE SIEGE**

a) – *A Fatal Meddling*

"*That the sow he was fattening fo' the wedding had already died,*" they notified a certain Jacinto Argüelles; to a Ramiro, from the village *"Las Margaritas,"* they required that *"he report to his home because a relative had passed away"*; to somebody else, they informed about the sale of some goats *"which were pending,"* and that his mother had arrived well from the trip. And the list of notices continued interminably, some of them truly comical and ingenuous. It was *"The Voice of the Tarahumara,"* in its section of messages. Based in a town south of the sierra, this station broadcasts news, music and advertising in Spanish and Rarámuri. For many remote communities it is the only means of communication, even though in the deepness of the canyons it is difficult to receive its signal. Thus happened in Gervasio's house, situated on the bottom of a narrow ravine. Muddled amongst the buzzing of static, some high-pitched little voices singing in Rarámuri in time to the monotonous chords of a violin could hardly be heard. When I asked the rarámuri to translate them his answer left me stunned, he didn't understand what they were saying; the singers were *"hueris,"* of the rarámuris *"who live up there on the sierra,"* and they spoke *"in another way,"* almost unintelligible to him. He turned the volume up and, along with his wife, he approached the loudspeaker trying to interpret the lyrics, but they only managed to comprehend some single words; for quite a long time both of them were making suppositions, laughing afterwards at the crazy ideas that occurred to them; finally they gave up, *"who knows what it says."*

That was the first time I realized the enormous diversity that exists within this millenarian ethnic group. Contrary to popular belief, the tarahumaras do not form a homogeneous group; the term is used to denominate some three or four subgroups of indigenous communities whose main bond of union is the geographic zone where they live; but they keep very important differences among themselves, like variations in the phonetics, the vocabulary and the grammar of the language, which make their intercommunication difficult and even impossible. They also differ in the way of dressing and the degree of acceptance of modern civilization that, regularly, is linked to the proximity of their hamlets to the mestizo population centers, and which has even disrupted the traditional values of their culture. Fortunately, due in part to these differences, and in spite of the suspicious interest of certain foreign groups, the tarahumaras have not acquired the false and pernicious overestimation of their ethnical identity that, induced by wicked external influences, have artificially developed other aboriginal groups like the huicholes, the seris or, even worse,

143

the kikapús; which, far from promoting racial unity and strengthening their moral values, has caused a disastrous prostitution of their cultures.

Nicolás was the typical tarahumara that had adapted to civilization. He was dressed like the mestizos: pants, shirt and hat cowboy style; and he only continued wearing the tire rubber sole huaraches, normally worn by the Indians, because shoes and boots were too tight for him; *"I can't find my size,"* he complained. His cracked feet had suffered the changes that a whole life of long walks causes: a wide and callous sole, and a huge big toe, separated from the other toes, prehensile and robust to give support to the walk and facilitate the ascent of slopes. He graduated as a teacher in one of the rural schools of the Instituto Nacional Indigenista (National Institute for the Indians) and had been principal of the shelter-school of his community, where he had also had positions of authority. Besides, he was a health promoter and in his house he had a little general store. After many *"troublesome"* procedures, he had achieved a goal that he had longed for: a position in the school of a nearby mestizo village of the canyons, which was about five hours of walking distance downstream; that's why he only went to his home on weekends. To avoid *"so much coming and going,"* he was planning to move his family there, and had already bought a lot *"to build."*

His eldest daughter had also studied to be a teacher, and married a mestizo of the village; she only visited them every once in a while, for a short time, because she didn't like the community much anymore; she got bored and life there seemed very hard. Her husband, on the contrary, loved this place and he got on well with the local natives, who frequently invited him to the tesgüinadas. In a beautiful golden evening, pointing at some spectacular rocky cirques that crowned the canyons, he said to me very enthusiastic: *"look at those huge stones so pretty! I'd like to live here and establish a large and well stocked store, not like the one of my father-in-law."*

Nicolás liked to collect family photos; he had a box full of them, all piled and dusty, some rolled up or torn, others crumpled and stained. Once he asked me to take a photograph of him, *"as a keepsake"*; when I realized he had already put his white uniform of health promoter on and, with the hair still wet, he posed in the yard of his house along with his family, also dressed hurriedly with their best clothes. One day he showed me the pictures of a trip they took to México City, when they were taken by an anthropologist who visits them periodically, bringing students to train them in field work. All the Indians appeared attired with a cloth band on the head, loose shirt and zapeta all in white, very clean and ironed, as I've never seen them in the Tarahumara; even Nicolás, who in the sierra dresses like a mestizo, wore the traditional clothing, with a surprising neatness. In some photographs the group of Indians danced in front of an audience of men wearing suits and elegant ladies; in others they were on a platform surrounded by a curious crowd, as if they were monkeys in some zoo; they were grotesque scenes. When I asked him what he had brought from the city, he answered laconically: *"nothing, they took us to know the place."* The lack of ethics and the irresponsibility of a supposedly scholar of human culture was outrageous; who, to gain favors, subjected the Indians to an intensive course of deculturization that did not contribute any benefit; exhibiting them like marionettes before a public who, more often than not, is insensitive and incapable of valuing the cultural richness of man.

Unfortunately, this is not the only case in which someone feels to have the right to disrupt the cultural integrity of the tarahumaras. Attracted by absurd myths born out of ignorance, odd chaps often arrive at the sierra searching for supernatural experiences. From the ingenuous who comes in hopes of meeting the *"tarahumaran supermen,"* to the show-off, who putting on some huaraches, a cloth band on the head and babbling some words in Rarámuri, pretends to be more tarahumara than the tarahumaras, and proclaims to have deciphered the essence of a mysterious and inaccessible philosophy that rules the life of the aborigines. These diverse stances are reflected in the extensive literature written on the theme; commencing with the texts that remind the debates of the beginning of the colonial epoch, where it was questioned if the Indians had a soul and if they could be considered human beings with capacity for reasoning; passing then by the formal studies that try to elucidate the cosmovision and mentality that regulate the behavior of the tarahumara, which sometimes try to pigeonhole them, to homogenize all of them within the same scheme of conduct, as if they were automatons incapable of reacting independently and creating their own ideas; denying, thus, one of the fundamental characteristics of the human being: the diversity of thought, which singles out his attitude facing life. At the other extreme are the authors who distort things to adapt them to their fantasies and idealize the Indian, considering him full of prodigious qualities and of an extraterrestrial sensibility that would confer him an esoteric wisdom, which would give him access to a secret supernatural redoubt banned for the rest of humankind. And there is no lack of someone who attributes an almost ideal perfection to him.

In reality, as any culture unique in its kind that develops in a fascinating natural environment to which it has managed to integrate in an extraordinary way, the tarahumaran society proves to be impassioning and enthralling, even amazing in some aspects; but it is, after all, human, with all the defects and virtues that such condition entails. This nowise takes the merit away; it simply gives things their true proportion. Isn't the adaptation of the Eskimos to the inclemencies of the Arctic, or the ability of the Amazonian tribes to unravel the natural secrets that enable them to survive amongst the dangers of the jungle, as amazing?

Throughout history, negative judgments of whites and mestizos against the Indians have been constant, in which a racist contempt is very patent. The first missionaries already considered them barbarians or animals, because their behavior didn't adapt to the patterns of conduct of the European of that epoch. The root of the problem is that the aborigine is judged with different and stricter parameters than those used to judge our own acts. His defects are exaggerated, dodging ours, to be able to justify our superiority complexes. But alcoholism, violence, ignorance and even stupidity, are common evils in any human group. Obfuscated by our absurd pretension of being better than them, we confuse the scientific achievements of a few with the general intellectual development. The truth is, that in spite of all the current technological sophistication, we can neither consider ourselves more intelligent nor wiser than, for instance, the Greek philosophers of thousands of years ago or the brilliant French thinkers of the pre-Revolutionary epoch; nor can modern artists brag of being more sensitive to beauty or have a better aesthetic sense than the great artists of the Renaissance. In fact our "advances" are based on very ancient inventions or discoveries, and in some aspects, we have not even surpassed the caveman.

In the tarahumaran society, just like in any other human society of all the earth and of all times, it is just a handful of individuals who concern themselves with finding a meaning to the human existence in the Universe, or that, disturbed by the closeness of Nature, marvel at its harmony and beauty, and try to find an explanation. For the vast majority life is only a succession of inert days, of nights without stars, of dormant souls that, guided by the instincts, only worry about knowing what they are going to eat, who they are going to marry, or what color of dress they are going to put on. It is indispensable to individualize because it is deceptive to evaluate man as a group. The actions of a few people are what condition the general consciousness and determine the course; the rest simply form a deplorable mass of manipulable and anonymous beings. Modern civilization has no reason to boast about its society being the best, or of having a superior intellect. The human being keeps being the same, no matter the epoch or the place; only the quality of his spirit uplifts him to the sublime or sinks him into bestiality.

book, dirty and with its pages ripped out, was lying on the ground amidst the mud of a puddle, in front of the door of a classroom. Unexpectedly, two tarahumara kids came out chasing themselves at top speed and inadvertently stepped on it on passing, tearing out a leaf which, carried by the wind, went swirling around in the middle of a cloud of dust toward the bottom of an adjacent ravine. Curious, I approached to read it; a photograph of Mussolini illustrated the first page. The text, in Spanish, was about the Second World War; the combats, the bombings, the massacres. The uselessness of knowing such atrocities in this isolated corner of the planet left me perplexed. What importance could it have in the life of the aborigine?

I was in a remote shelter-school, near the profundities of an intricate defile. It was the Instituto Nacional Indigenísta which built this kind of institutions of basic education in strategic places of the sierra; here the students of the scattered tarahumaran hamlets are concentrated to give them maintenance and lodging during the days of classes, sending them back to their homes on weekends. Some students live almost a day's walking distance away, going up the sheer walls of the canyons.

It was Saturday and, however, there were more than ten children playing in the yards and the dormitories. They were dressed traditionally and spoke in Rarámuri; one could only talk in Spanish with some of the older ones, with difficulty. On a rudimentary basketball court, devoid of an adequate ball, a couple of kids tried to score a basket with an improvised ball of rolled paper, bouncing it against the deteriorated backboards. At noon, they all gathered in the kitchen to make the dinner because it was the cook's day off. While some of them brought the firewood for the adobe stove, others prepared a noodle soup; the naughtiest spent time joking, throwing little bits of tortilla at one another, or smearing beans on their faces. A tremendous series of shouts and guffaws, accompanied by a dense cloud of smoke, announced that the meal had burned. The principal had to come put things in order, admonishing them in moderation. Disheartened, he explained that the children only stayed because they knew that they would eat better there than in their homes, and besides, they could have a good time with their friends. He could not deny them food and force them to leave, *"if one scolds them, they leave and don't come back for several weeks."* Sometimes, he had had to go get them, but normally the parents themselves are who send them back, when their presence begins to be a burden for the family budget; *"they just send them for us to support them."* This attitude, apparently negative, and the lack of interest in the school education of children, turn out logical if we consider that for the Indian this education has no real usefulness. It is practically impossible for a tarahumara to gain access to a higher level of education and finish a profession; first of all, due to lack of economic resources. What he could aspire to the most, if he managed to obtain a scholarship from the *"INI,"* would be to become a bilingual rural teacher and practice in a community distant from his, where, in addition to losing his familial bonds, his meager salary would barely be enough to give him the same economic low level of living he already has. It's common to meet dissatisfied teachers due to the remoteness of their work places; they live yearning for their homeland, and seize the slightest opportunity to go visit it, suspending classes.

In the rarámuri society, education is essentially a practical experience, children learn following the example of their parents. The adaptation of the tarahumara to his environment begins since the earliest stages of his existence, and, due to the difficult conditions of life, only those with greater aptitudes to face them, manage to survive. The child is left free once he is capable of walking, and while playing he frolics at the edge of hair-raising abysses, sharing life with dogs, goats and hens. Growing in intimate contact with Nature, he learns in an elementary way to submit to discipline. Among tries and falls; among pricks and wounds, he gains experience and understands the world that surrounds him. This instills into his mind the humility of obedience and the acceptance of his limitations.

At about ten years of age the child is completely autonomous; he knows his environment perfectly well, and is capable of moving around it in full safety. The parents delegate some responsibilities to him that are important for the family, like grazing livestock or providing the water, which regularly must be brought from distant places, in large pots. Since the time that he is a little boy, he exerts a lot of physical activity in all his games, which include exhausting races, wrestling and strength competitions that stimulate muscular development and which, on becoming an adult, enable him to transport heavy loads, travel long distances at surprising speeds and ascend abrupt precipices with an unusual facility. His adaptation to the sierra is absolute.

Generally, it is considered that on being sixteen years old, the youth is prepared to lead an independent life, for he has sufficient capacity to work and reproduce, and he knows how to assume responsibilities and make decisions. The indigenous adolescent does not have the grave problems of social maladjustment of the adolescents of modern society, who, after growing with great dependence and isolated in an artificial environment where parents try to protect them from any harm or lack of anything, are, suddenly, exposed to the real world, hostile and unknown, which they don't know how to face because, spurred by mass propaganda, they claim rights are granted without responsibilities. Life is extremely difficult for the Indian, and his youth must prepare to face it.

From the moment the tarahumara child is obliged to leave his home to attend school, they are denying him the possibility of acquiring the traditional knowledge that would serve him to survive in the environment where he lives. School education, theoretical and inappropriate, does not offer him a true option to improve, preserving his ancestral legacy. When they try to impose a foreign lifestyle and language on him, they make an attempt on his cultural integrity because the child's mentality is negatively affected, damaging the fundamental structure of this millenarian society. The child is victim of a silent cultural spoliation that returns nothing to him in exchange, condemning him even to forget his typical sports. In the tarahumara communities near the mestizo villages the students are frequently sent to study in the local school, accelerating the loss of their customs because, subjected to the mockery of their non indigenous classmates, they end up ashamed even of wearing their traditional clothing. The rarámuri teachers, forced to study far from their homes, know well this degrading experience.

The problem is so serious that numerous teachers disagree with the official policy. The most daring modify the syllabus according to their discretion, taking advantage of the fact that supervisors hardly arrive to these isolated places. The majority of the teachers are tarahumaras who still have their culture deeply rooted and preserve their traditions. Many of them own parcels of land and depend on their crops to complement their income to be able to subsist. It is common that in key seasons of the agricultural cycle they suspend classes to attend their cultivations, and send the pupils back to their homes so that they can help their parents in farm work. This gives rise to harsh criticism from the mestizo teachers of the federal school system, who, showing a worrying ignorance of the problem, underestimate their work, considering they are badly prepared and do not contribute any benefit to education.

Such is the deplorable situation of the indigenous education system that, without a coherent and realistic plan that takes into account the life conditions of the Indian, his culture and idiosyncrasy; lacking qualified personnel that is truly interested in helping and respecting the tarahumara; and stagnated by corruption and bureaucratic ineptitude, ends up being frankly deculturizing. Even the new bilingual programs have a limited perspective of the cultural respect and do not consider measures to strengthen the ethnic identity of each group; which is comprehensible on visiting the administrative offices of the system, where there are all sorts of things except Indians; well, only in paintings, hanging from the walls. There, strategies are developed and activities organized to *"educate"* the indigenous people and *"get them out of their terrible ignorance and backwardness."* In recent years alleged reforms to the institution *"responsible for the development of the indigenous people"* were decreed; unfortunately, as it usually happens with the government departments, in the end, all that changed was the name.

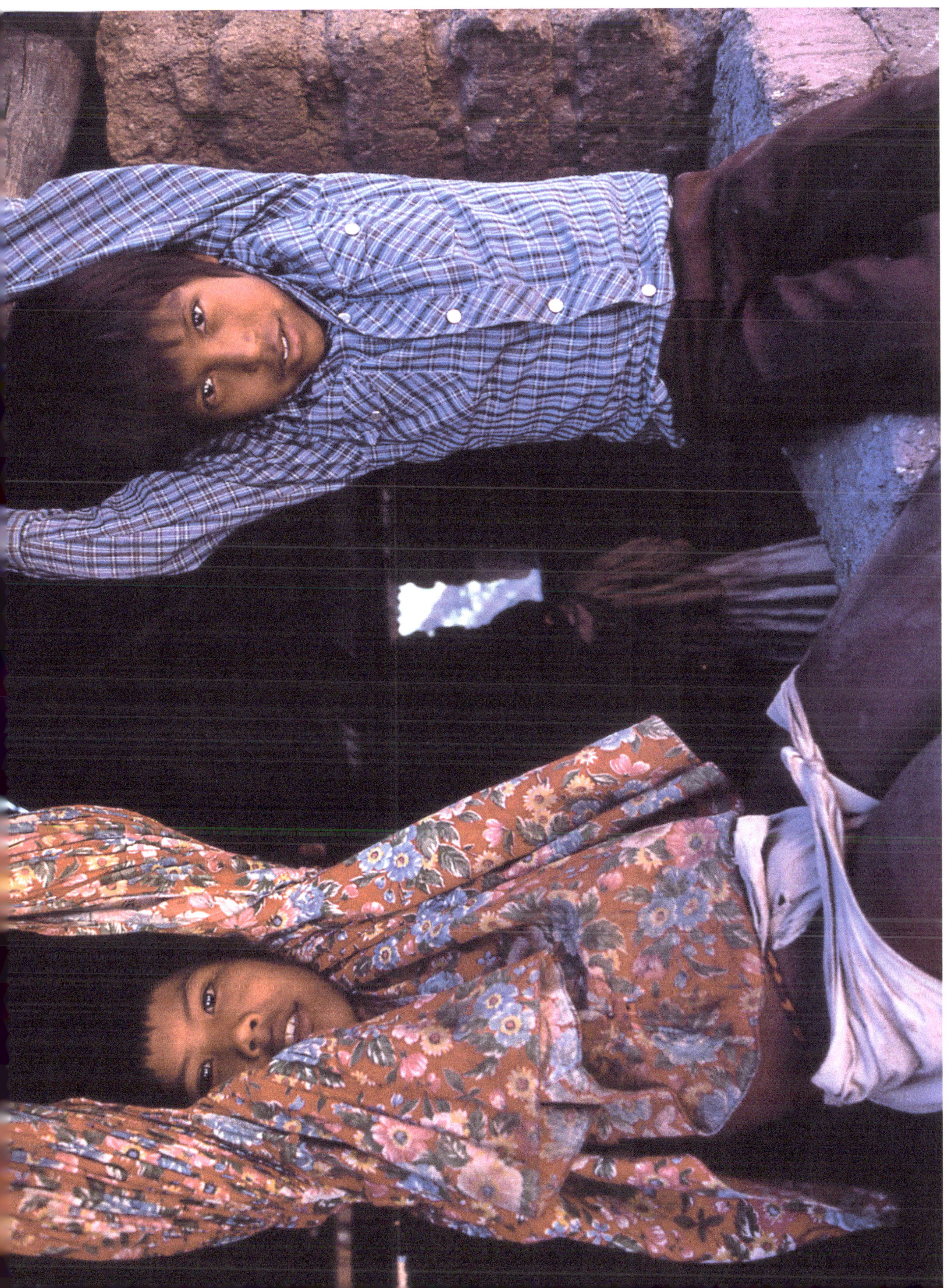

This obsolete and paternalistic approach has its root in past epochs, when, on being born the independent México, it was considered of vital importance to create a nationalist consciousness, to unify the Mexicans and protect the country against the risk of foreign invasions. The existence of small divergent cultural groups, like the ethnic groups, was seen as an obstacle to attain the national integration, and it was necessary to eliminate them. It was said that the Indians didn't have a consciousness of nationality and, if they persisted in preserving their culture, they could not be Mexicans. The education system was conceived as the most suitable instrument to vanish them within a short time, incorporating them gradually into the supposed prototype of the national culture, represented by the mestizo. The most derisory is that, far from being a threat to Mexicanity, the presence of autochthonous groups is one of its primordial constituents for the enormous costumbrist and ideological contribution with which they have helped to forge the cultural richness of our nation; and it should be a great source of pride. The true strength of a country does not increase with the denial of its historical legacy, but with the ability of its citizens to understand and adapt themselves to the immeasurable diversity of Nature.

Elpidio constituted a rare case; he was the only mestizo, that I knew, working as the person in charge of an indigenous shelter. He didn't even speak Tarahumara; he had learned some words though, *"just to gab with the cooks,"* who every other minute *"stubbornly insisted"* on teaching him to speak it. When I expressed my belief that only bilingual Indians were hired for these positions, he concernedly explained to me that there were not enough qualified personnel among them, *"they don't find people, they're not interested in preparing themselves"*; and he expounded on the situation of the head of a shelter who spent all the time drinking until lying drunk in the school yard or in the classrooms, neglecting his functions. I believed him; I had recently spent a week in that community and I couldn't talk with the man in charge; I never found him sober. Disheartened, he said this was not an isolated occurrence, and to that he added the inconsistency of the teachers to perform their work, causing *"a real mess"* in the educational system.

A month after his arrival, Elpidio had done notable improvements to the facilities: he replaced broken window glasses and blown out light bulbs; he built a cement wash basin and, with hoses, he supplied it with water, facilitating the washing of clothes; he also installed a water faucet in the kitchen, *"for not struggling with making meals,"* and put to work a rustic gas stove which had been dumped in a corner, winning the gratitude of the cooks. The cleanliness of the place was another of his priorities, and he had imposed a stricter discipline to teach the children to respect the class timetable and carry out the daily chores; *"they have them accustomed to do just as they please,"* he said annoyed, disapproving the attitude of former directors. When the teachers didn't come he *"entered to help"* so that the pupils did not stop studying, although, not being a bilingual teacher, he was limited to only a *"few things"* he could teach them and resigned himself to making them draw letters or to entertain themselves by *"viewing the little figures of the books."* He felt sorry that they only came to waste their time *"frolicking in the courts,"* after so many hours of arduous walking that left them exhausted and panting; above all, the youngest students, who could hardly keep the pace of the older ones and often lagged behind; he had seen them arrive half an hour later, crying. If he learned the teachers were going to leave *"to perform a commission"* for several days, he *"flatly"* notified the parents so that they didn't send their children and would rather have them stay at their houses to help them. Sarcastically, he lamented there were adolescents in the fifth and sixth grades of elementary school who didn't even know how to write their name, as they had been promoted to the higher grades based only on their height; angrily, he concluded: *"they should at least teach them to read, so they can defend themselves."*

With a squat body and a very short height, he wore a thick mustache that gave him a severe aspect, contrasting with his cheerful nature and his easy and pleasant manner. Of humble background, with difficulty, he managed to finish high school; although he considered he had learned more in *"the school of life."* For some time he went as a *"wetback"* to the United States, until he got interested in the indigenous questions, actively participating in several institutions dedicated to help them. Once they even confused him with a rarámuri, inviting him with a group of tarahumaras to attend a great reunion of indigenous people of the continent, which was performed on *"the other side"*; thrilled, he praised the perfect organization of the event and the enormous chances they gave them to cross the border *"without passport or anything else."* He was fascinated by the magnificence of the Powwow. His relationship with the Indians oscillated between a frank rejection to their culture, product of the prejudices of his mestizoan education, and a discreet admiration for their extraordinary capacity to survive in such critical conditions, which provoked in him a sincere compassion for the children, the principal affected ones by their very bad economic situation. He always asked me to take them sweaters or jackets to protect them from the tremendous winter cold, *"it doesn't matter they are secondhand, of those that are sold there in the flea markets."*

Ever since he was young, he had liked *"being knowing,"* and together with some friends he had explored some parts of the sierra. One night he related to me several intriguing finds. Guided by a tarahumara, they discovered a monumental cavern to which they entered crawling through an extremely narrow crack; to illuminate the interior they lit improvised torches of branches causing the stampede of hundreds of bats, *"millions"* said he, which in their crazy flight crashed against their bodies, making them scream with panic while they advanced sinking their feet and slipping on a viscous layer of guano that covered the ground. When the calm returned they noticed that at one of the ends of the cave there was a sort of altar and, at the other, several benches in a row which had been carved directly on the rock of the walls; there were also three large holes *"like doorways,"* each of them leading to a *"room"* where, terrified, they found some skeletons. Apparently, subsequent studies determined that the place could have served as a refuge for Jesuit missionaries, who refused to abandon the Tarahumara during the exile, *"or maybe in the epoch of the cristeros* (Christ Fighters)*."*

On another excursion they found a cave with the entrance sealed with clay and stones, some of which had crumbled owing to the rains leaving a hole toward the inside; on illuminating it with a flashlight they discovered several indigenous mummies sitting in a circle. They were very well preserved, with their long hair and their shriveled eyes in the back of their sunken sockets; they seemed to be celebrating a solemn meeting, looking at one another *"as if they were talking."* Unfortunately, thrilled by the discovery, they notified the authorities, and it didn't take long for the scientist to come to disturb their eternal sleep. Amazed at the exceptional process of mummification, which they attributed to the singular porosity of the soil, and disconcerted by the strange postures the bodies kept, they considered a more meticulous study, necessary. They took them out of the merciful enclosure where those who loved them tried to protect them; and, without asking permission, they took them to cloister in a museum.

And then that enigmatic story of a respectable merchant of a nearby town, who with great vehemency swore to have been carried by Martians, together with his wife, to a fantastic sidereal voyage, to show them their world. They were out of the earth for a week. The convincing similarity of the accounts of both spouses, even in the smallest details, *"as if they were seeing them"*; the coincidence of a rare and unexpected disappearance of the couple during that time, corroborated by relatives and friends; and the remarkable consistency of their detailed and eloquent narrations in spite of the passage of many years and continual repetition, seemed to support the authenticity of the event; added to that, the prestige and earnestness of these people, now already elderly, whose honesty was unquestionable. In view of the overwhelming firmness of such arguments, their surprised neighbors were left *"with the 'Jesus' in their mouth,"* caught in the awkward dilemma of believing or not such an implausible story. Scratching one of his ears from behind, confounded, Elpidio finished asking me: *"ya, how do ya see it?"*

One afternoon, on returning from an exhausting journey, I encountered a large group of pupils taking a bath in the river; it was the day for personal cleanliness. Near the shore, putting another of his numerous skills into practice, Elpidio had improvised a barbershop in the open air sitting the children on a *"balled"* stone, to cut their hair quite short, almost shaved, before allowing them to go swim. To his feet the sand was covered with locks of hair, which the gusts of wind scattered through the air; *"now we really sent the nits to fly,"* he said satisfied. Already with the hair short, the youngsters got excited on detecting little bugs creeping on their head; when they informed *"the barber,"* he urged them strongly, *"then, what are you waiting for? Kill them!"* Making a big racket, the kids sat next to the water and, between shouts and guffaws, they were there a long time squeezing one another's heads, to gut the lice.

If she abandoned her husband it was because he was the sterile. Since she was a child they had instilled in her that infertility and abortion were sin, and she wanted to get pregnant to escape the menace of any hidden curse; that was why she went with another man, to form a family. But it didn't take long for the husband to find her and went choleric to complain. After several violent incidents, the lady decided to seek the help of the governor of the community to solve her problem. After pondering the question conscientiously, the leader resolved that the woman's reasons were valid; she was within her right to want to have children. Nevertheless, she had to compensate the husband for the loss. After discussing with the couple some possibilities, they reached an agreement to give the plaintiff a few domestic animals to settle and close the dispute. The husband was satisfied with the exchange of the wife for a cow and a bunch of goats. They never talked about the matter again.

Ever since the ancient epoch in which the missionaries instituted in the pastoral centers a new system of command, headed by the governors, they have helped to settle disputes amongst the members of their communities and served as liaison with the mestizoan authorities. This governing structure fit so well in the indigenous mentality that, out of convenience, it was widely fostered by the Jesuit religious, and has lasted up to the present day. Every community is ruled by a triad of governors, one general and two secondaries, supported by a group of officers who perform various functions. The requisites for the selection of candidates are very simple and common; any responsible and honest person can have access to these posts, which entail a great commitment and work since, unlike our rulers, they do really act like true public servants. Although these leaders do not rely on weapons or on penal codes to assert their authority, they have traditionally had an enormous moral power and are highly respected by their people. The decisions of the government are taken jointly, and it is normal for the community to participate in them. In the indigenous conception of justice, compensation for damages caused is more desirable than punishment of the offender. However, the interaction with modern civilization has influenced the tarahumara ideology more than many would like to accept.

Invited by an old acquaintance to a tesgüinada, in the evening I climbed half the slope of an abrupt ravine to reach, exhausted and sweaty, the small terrace where his house was. A large group of guests held a lively conversation around several big pots brimming with tesgüino. Since my arrival I noticed a heavy atmosphere of aggressiveness among the participants. An old man dressed in the traditional style kept arguing with the host; he was upset by the presence of some tarahumaras who, by their clothes, resembled mestizos. I knew that man well, he was a traditionalist to the bone who, in spite of having a good friendship with me for having treated him of his illnesses, he detested the tarahumaras who accepted, without a qualm, the western civilization, which he considered harmful to the rarámuris. This time alcohol made him more irascible and intolerant. The governor, who was also dressed like a mestizo, intervened to calm him, admonishing him impatiently in Spanish: *"why do you make such a fuss if we are all from the same."* Frustrated and sad, the old man sighed deeply and went to sit by my side; shaking his head discreetly, he approached my ear and said in a low voice: *"it's not true; it's not true."*

It was for me the first sign of a grave crack in the indigenous soul. In the course of the years I could differentiate three phases of a gradual process of decomposition which not only affects the tarahumaras but also all the ethnic groups of the country. The traditionalists, mostly elderly, try to preserve their customs taking shelter in the inaccessible sierras, struggling against adversity. On the opposite extreme are the aborigines who have permanently emigrated to the cities relegating their culture and forgetting their origin. Between both of them there is a majority group that has not found such a simple answer; even though they are proud of their indigenous heritage, they have accepted some modern innovations to facilitate their existence. Here are included many teachers who since they were young were separated from their families and, wrapped in a strange environment, ended up distancing themselves so much from their ancestors that they don't know many of their traditions and it is common to hear them speak of *"they"* as if they belonged to a foreign and unknown culture.

In it one also finds some leaders who, unfortunately, have become corrupted. A good example was that of a governor who frequently went *"on honeymoon"* to the city with one of his several wives, using to his advantage the resources the state contributed to his community. Nonetheless, in his sermons he extolled their traditions and values, charging against the mestizos; *"they have a lot to learn from us,"* he proclaimed ostentatiously. Once, after another boastful speech, I asked him why, if he loathed them, he dressed like them and owned a truck; he didn't know what to reply, he looked at me angrily and left in a choppy mood. His malice and cynicism were, to me, something new and repugnant.

Of course, there exist those who seek to give a positive approach to the problem. An illustrative example is the attitude of a group of indigenous governors who participated in a meeting with the papal representative in this country. Pleased, they thanked him for his interest in helping them,

but at the same time they respectfully requested his intercession to reduce the massive and disturbing meddling of the civilization on their people; making it clear that they didn't require big road or urbanistic projects, nor sophisticated technologies like television. For them, a battery-operated radio was more than enough. With a charming humility, full of profound logic and wisdom, they explained to him: *"we don't need so many things to live."*

During the last three centuries, and in particular after the exile of the Jesuits, a veiled and wicked labor to debilitate the authority of the governors has been carried out, distorting and underestimating their fundamental principles, creating serious conflicts on the inside of this ancestral culture. According to official declarations, it is inadmissible to concede the Indians the right to govern themselves under an autochthonous system of law, since giving them autonomy would be equivalent to allowing the existence of a country within another, compromising the integrity of the nation. I still remember vividly the entrancing emotion of my first encounter with a tarahumara dressed in his traditional attire; he was a robust young man who ran swiftly on a green plateau, with his loose shirt in vibrant colors flapping in the wind. His athletic figure stood out against the blue of a sky filled with clouds of immaculate whiteness; he seemed the living image of freedom personified. While he approached, I imagined him armed with a bow and arrow, disposed to attack me, and I understood the dread of the first colonists on confronting such a formidable foe. Ironically, I had the pleasant and perturbing impression of having arrived at another country, where a language that was incomprehensible to me was spoken, and the clothing and customs were very distinct from mine; but, above all, a place where the meaning of life and the way of enjoying it, were totally different and inconceivable for a consumeristic mentality like ours. Even more, I had the odd sensation of having been taken back in time, moving back all of a sudden to an ancient epoch in which the natural laws ruled the human existence.

Before this palpable reality, the official stance proves absurd and reveals a tremendous ignorance, aggravated by an alarming negligence to learn the true state of the problem, trying to resolve it with impractical office solutions. For more than five hundred years in the indigenous territories their ancestral laws have been in force without it having undermined the authority of the government or fragmented the country. The indigenous demand is very sensible, they are simply asking to give legality to a condition that in fact exists since centuries ago; thus they could defend themselves from the arbitrary actions of the mestizos, like the spoliation of their land or the irrational depredation of their natural resources which does not bring them any benefit. A negative response to this petition only demonstrates a shameful racism and, even worse, a strategy of extermination which conceals shady deals with the local political bosses who for an immemorial time have exploited the ethnic groups. The creation of indigenous states which, as participants of an effective federalism, could be ruled by their own laws within a more flexible and conciliatory legal framework, which takes into account the ideological diversity of the

country without discrediting anybody, would strengthen our cultural heritage and would allow the autochthonous minorities to preserve their cultural traits and way of life, requiring minimal support to stabilize their economic conditions.

The tarahumaras have based their relationship with modern society on their own rules of coexistence, but they have not been reciprocated. Their goodwill has been confused with idiocy, their idea of mutual respect with cowardice, and their desire to preserve their ancient customs with ignorance. They have waited in vain for a favorable response. On feeling betrayed they have obliged themselves to change in order to counteract the damage and try to survive, many of them with a dormant rancor in their heart. Unfortunately, there does not seem to be a possible return; the transformation that the indigenous culture is undergoing, even in its fundamental parts, is undeniable. The thesis that their ideology has remained unaltered in spite of so many centuries of external influence is untenable, and the argument that a tarahumara of yesteryear wouldn't have difficulty in recognizing his present descendants is ridiculous. It suffices to look at the tarahumara teachers who, dressed like mestizos, follow the latest fashion in haircut and clothing, carry sophisticated disc players and proudly drive automotive vehicles, and have learned to measure time, trapping their lives in the relentless ticking of the hands of a watch. What would their ancient kind think of them?

I had been lodged in the dispensary of the school of a remote hamlet in the canyons for several days; sleeping by night on a ramshackle sofa whose intimidating squeaking populated my rest with nightmares, in which I plunged terrified towards the invisible bottom of a sinister and gloomy precipice, in which I never finished falling. Consultation was scarce and in the meager medicine chest there barely were a few analgesic tablets, antidiarrheal suspensions and *"something fo' the mange."* One afternoon I got myself to play with the students of the shelter, inventing competitions and riddles that I rewarded with candies and dried fruit; let's see who climbs up higher on that tree, who throws a wooden ball with the foot better, or who makes the drum resound more powerfully, moistening with mouthfuls of water or saliva the leather drumheads *"to tighten them more strongly"* and increase their resonance; habit learned from the adults, though these ones preferred to use tesgüino. Unexpectedly, two teenagers completely inebriated approached demanding, aggressively, that I give them food because they were hungry; they went so far as to try to snatch the sweets, frightening the small children due to the struggle. Although the boys knew me well, because I frequented their community and I had treated their relatives, under the influence of alcohol, their complexes and frustrations came out into the open; they had lived in the city where they suffered wrongs and maltreatments. I was the symbol of the civilization that had caused so many damages to their people, and they wanted to get back at me for their profound resentment. It was, perhaps, my bitterest and most unpleasant and depressing experience in the sierra. To try to calm them down and prevent a serious confrontation, I threatened to send for the governor; their revealing reply was full of contempt: *"call him, we're not afraid of him anyway; lousy governor he's good for nothing."*

Farther beyond all was darkness and mystery; a vast realm unknown and fascinating, land of insoluble enigmas that unleashed the imagination filling the soul with fantasies. The world was limited to the brief space that the flickering flame of the bonfire managed to illuminate. The immobile silhouettes of two tarahumara old men sitting by the fire resembled spectral creatures who had escaped from obscurity, and whose whispering mingled with the soft crackling of the firewood. Above us, high up in the firmament, nebulae and galaxies majestically crossed the magnificent infinity of the sidereal space, where, defenseless, the tremulous twinkling of the multicolored stars, which seemed to beat in harmony with the heart, was wrecked. The Universe flooded the night with a strange gleam that made us dream.

In the distance, on the horizon, the gloomy immensity of the canyons, swamped with silence, was barely discernable. Several luminous dots appeared suddenly, incrusted into the sheer walls like tiny lanterns that, hanging precariously over the abyss, tried in vain to dissipate that imposing sea of shadows; they were bonfires just lit which, tearing the black gag that rendered the earth mute, disclosed the presence of other isolated hamlets in which people took refuge to forget their archaic nocturnal fear; unfortunate legacy of the first human being. It was an impressive sight; it seemed impossible that someone dared to live in such an inhospitable place. And there were again the dormant dinosaurs, covered with a thick layer of luminescent mist, impassible before our disquietude. It all seemed to be a dream, an uncertain memory from the past that infused the terrifying and enthralling feeling of being contemplating the birth of the landscape, the primeval setting of the invention of the world, lost in the most hidden confines of the planet; a fleeting vision of the crucial moment in which, overwhelmed by fear, confusion and helplessness, the human mind created God.

Pedro wanted me to go see his parents before leaving, and to get to their house we had walked more than an hour since nightfall, lighted by a faint luminosity that filtered between the dark branches of the trees, making the twisting course of the path glisten with an unusual whiteness Surrounded by blackness we advanced slowly, uneasy and captivated at the same time by the proximity of the night, which we could almost touch on stretching out our arms. The lunar disc was merely a thin silvery curve that in my rapture I imagined as a split in the sphere of the heavens, as if a jet-black cloak that wrapped the earth would have ripped, disclosing a magnificent world filled with light which for time immemorial would have lain hidden behind the sky spangled with stars. When we arrived to the protection of the bonfire our archaic fears vanished. Immersed in such a majestic place, under the influence of the faint amber light and the grave nocturnal stillness, a rare facet of life was unexpectedly revealed, an unknown profundity in which time elapsed placidly and things became simple and diaphanous. In this unwonted reality, forgotten by modern man, in that intimate and total contact with Nature, the individual learns humility on realizing his insignificance and smallness, taking him to a profound communion of his spirit with the Cosmos where existence finds its true meaning. It was so easy, then, to reach happiness…

In the remote and primitive territory inhabited by the Indian there are no magic buttons that on pressing them invent electric light, packing the space with their dazzling brightness and destroying the charm of perceiving, hidden in the penumbra, the disturbing presence of a secret and impenetrable domain populated by intangible beings who, slipping furtively around us, spy on our lives. Here converge peace, fecund solitude and Nature, soul's liberating elements, creating a mythic and fantasious ambiance that overflows the senses and entrances thought, making the ephemeral passage of man on earth more exciting and enchanting.

That time my stay had prolonged to nearly three months, and I had fully entered into the slow rhythm of the Tarahumara; that leisurely cadence that takes us back to earlier times, when human life kept pace with the sun and the stars, when the moon filled the nights with romanticism; an unknown dimension of time that is so exasperating and alien for the inhabitants of the cities, that are trapped in the frantic race of savage modernism, without goals or meaning. Upon my departure from the sierra the news from the outside was devastating: earthquakes in Asia, war in Europe, epidemics in Africa… I had the impression of having been suspended in time; banished in some immutable corner of the globe where the past remained latent. The present civilization with all its technology supposedly indispensable, vital, could have collapsed, exterminated itself in a horrific suicidal holocaust, and in this isolated place the *"outmoded"* tarahumara society would have continued, imperturbable, its timeless cycle of life, attached to the natural laws.

The modern man has lost the notion of the harmony of the Universe and in his confusion he has insisted on creating an alleged better world, an artificial world that has distanced him from Nature. Before this unreasoned tendency, it is very significant that human groups which struggle to keep their simple way of life still exist, with millenary customs and traditions, clinging tenaciously to *"The Mother Earth."* Time has demonstrated the terrifying ravages that the technological *"advance"* has caused to the planet and the human being himself. If evolving is improving, the so celebrated current concept of *"progress"* turns out to be more and more false and absurd because, in fact, we are undergoing a real regression. The abuse of technology has provoked a lamentable detriment of the physical and intellectual faculties with which man is endowed. Whilst in the country a person advanced in years leads an active and productive life, it is much more probable that in the city he lives disabled, overwhelmed by diseases. This deterioration is fostered from the first stages of growth. While the tarahumara child enjoys

enormous independence and helps the maintenance of the family, the city child lives secluded between plastics and cement, defenseless before the unpunished manipulation of the mind by mass communication media, which limit and even nullify his capacity of reflection, transforming him into a consumeristic robot. The most terrible consequence is the irremediable death of the soul, which denies the individual the possibility of taking consciousness of his own existence in a real universe which is indispensable for the full development of the physical, mental and spiritual potentials of the human being, and which takes him to discover an intense and transcendental way of living that the civilized man does not even suspect anymore that it exists. It would be necessary to teach him again to feel heady with the fragrance of the forests, to fill with rapture in the immensity of the mountains, to dream under the stars.

The problems the indigenous groups face are a central topic of numerous conferences and reunions of all sorts of *"specialists,"* who try to solve them without taking into account the affected ones, as if they were mentally retarded people incapable of forging their own destiny. It proves sarcastic to discover that the study of these most ancient societies, governed by solid natural precepts with full force to this day, could contribute ideas to solve the ridiculous complications of modern life; and take up again the path towards a true evolution. A clean environment; a healthy family that give emotional stability and permit the physical and mental development of the children; a pattern of coexistence that provide personal and economical security to all the members of a society, with a mechanism to facilitate their interaction and achieve their acceptance and recognition, are fundamental parts of any social structure. There are essential principles with universal and perennial validity, whose observance is indispensable to keep our human quality; they were once interpreted as sacred laws, but such a concept, today, would be opprobrious for our pedantic modernist ideology packed with science, which has transformed us into demigods with the right to manipulate the world at our whim.

The ideal solution to the indigenous problem would be to give them back their land and let them live respecting their culture, which has so vigorous roots that it has persisted until today in spite of the irrational assailment of civilization to annihilate it. But this is an unthinkable utopia for a society sick with arrogance, accustomed to discredit the opposite ideas. Owing to the abysmal cultural gap, they try to analyze the indigenous mentality and behavior from our limited perspective, without molding the thought to the conditions the tarahumara faces; considering he could only be integrated into our society if he discards his values, ideology and feelings, for his culture is obsolete in our pompous space age. But it should be understood that not all of us wish a world full of computers and cell phones, of prodigious technological achievements and interplanetary voyages. It is not a sacrilege to try to rationalize *"progress."* There are still people who dream of a kind and serene life through which we can walk slowly, enjoying each step, and which allows us to liberate the spirit in order to find pleasure in the unfathomable mystery of existence. Fortunately, there are still people who, simply, wish to have a human life on earth.

Plunged into a morbid addiction to violence, depravation and the grotesque, modern civilization has engaged in a senseless fight against itself, slicing off the soul of the people, domesticating them, for the purpose of uniforming their way of acting, feeling, thinking; incapable of preserving the planet, and coexisting with other beings with whom it shares it, it has condemned itself to live in a painful and somber journey whose only objective is the accumulation of material possessions. Nevertheless, the infinite variety of the Universe cannot be confined within the narrow reach of our complexes. Homogenization leads irremediably to mediocrity, as it is already patent in our society which, boasting of its license disguised as liberalism, regards with indolence the vices, the degeneration and stupidity that are corrupting it. Before the grandeur of Cosmos it is not possible to brag about our spiritual misery.

To the contrary of the primitive people, who tend to differentiate clearly amongst the lazy, the irresponsible, the depraved, the wicked or the idiot, giving to each one their corresponding place, in the modern world they try to deny the individual differences established by Nature, pretending that all the people are equal. They speak until satiety about the rights of man, without ever mentioning the obligations one must fulfill in order to be considered as such. It is urgent to make a Universal Declaration of the Human Duties in which the respect for the earth and the natural laws must be cardinal points. In our derisible eagerness of wanting to humanize ourselves beyond the human, we have ended up dehumanizing ourselves. The diversity of ideas, of beings, of environments, of dreams, is an indispensable part of life because in it creativity emerges and the intellect develops. The present world's inclination towards globalization has increased pressure on the ethnic groups that try to keep themselves out to preserve their own identity; this attack against their independence, which is nothing less than a veiled attempt to exterminate them, only demonstrates the grave imbecility we suffer. The existence of different cultures corroborates the great divergence of human thought and is, in its essence, the purest expression of the liberty of man.

It's been centuries since the natural equilibrium was broken. The Indians most deeply rooted in their traditions, fight the last battle taking refuge in their remote homeland; refusing to integrate with civilization in spite of their critical situation. The day they disappear, their fascinating cultural legacy will be lost forever; legacy which began to decay since the distant times when the civilized man came to taint the noble land where the rarámuri lives, where the rarámuri dies…